The Insider's Guide for High School Students

A Handbook for the Ninth Grade Year

Also by Tim Healey and Alex Carter:

The Insider's Guide to High School
A Parent's Guide for the Ninth Grade Year
(Vandamere Press, 2010)

The Insider's Guide for High School Students

A Handbook for the Ninth Grade Year

Tim Healey and Alex Carter

St. Petersburg, Florida

Published by
Vandamere Press
P.O. Box 149
St. Petersburg, FL 33731
USA

ISBN: 978-0-918339-75-1

This book is dedicated to our parents:

To Sandra Carter, for always teaching and pushing me to excel; to David Carter, for knowing when to challenge me and when to accept me for who I am; to Suzie Carter, for your kind wishes and enduring patience with my father; and, to Pam Thompson, for always supporting me and believing in what I do; and, to Jerry Thompson, for being a true friend, golf buddy, and all-around great guy.

—Alex Carter

In memory of my parents: Vera & Ed Healey. My mother loved and supported me as only a mother can … no matter what I did. My father taught me the valuable skills of keeping life in perspective and treating all people the right way. I also dedicate this book to Ron and Gray Bryan, my supportive in-laws. These two amazing people have welcomed me into their family and taught me how to have faith in those you love.

—Tim Healey

Acknowledgements

This book was inspired by the countless parents who responded so positively to our first book, *The Insider's Guide to High School: A Parent's Handbook for the Ninth Grade Year.* We heard so often that as much as they appreciated the insights and advice from our book, they continued to struggle in conversations about high school with their teens. They complained that after reading a chapter they were full of ideas, but their teen was still "in the dark." They asked, "Why don't you write a companion book for our teen to read at the same time as we are reading the parent's handbook?" "What a great idea!" we thought. Thanks to all the parents that suggested we do something that should have been so obvious to us in the first place.

Our undying gratitude goes to our families: Nickie, Tim's wife, and Mathew, Elizabeth, and Andrew, Tim's children; and, Wendy, Alex's wife, and Anna and Reid, Alex's children. Without their support and willingness to release us from our most important commitments on nights and weekends, we could never have finished this project. Also, our thanks go to our number one proofreader, Sandra Carter.

We would also like to thank our amazing publishing house, Vandamere Press; and the unflagging support of our publisher Art Brown, our editor Pat Berger, and our designer Victor Weaver.

A special thanks to our friends and supporters: Karyn Riddle, Larry Pullen, Mary Rubadeau, Andrew Massaro, Chris Neubauer, Mike Holupka, Steve Walts, Rae Darlington; Wendy Fulton; Brian Beaty; Geoff and Paula Polglase; and Rob Thorne.

Finally, we would like to acknowledge the thousands upon thousands of young men and women we have had the honor and pleasure of working with over the years as high school principals. Without their fine examples and inspiration we would have had nothing to write about! Thanks to all of you.

Table of Contents

Introduction

Fast forward to a beautiful sunny day in late May or early June. The sky is crystal blue. There are a few puffy white clouds scattered across the horizon, and the temperature is just right. The sun's warmth feels good on your face. All across America, seventeen, eighteen, and nineteen year old students graduate from high school on days just like this one. In four short years, you will be graduating too!

Everybody is happy on graduation day. Students are excited, yet a little bit nervous, to be leaving high school and moving on to continue their formal educations at colleges, universities, or technical training centers. Perhaps they will be starting a career or joining the military to serve their country. Parents and families are happy because they are proud to see their "child" walk across the stage and receive a diploma. Teachers are happy because they know that they have helped these students grow up and mature from nervous, unsure ninth-graders to prepared, confident citizens ready for adulthood. Principals are happy because everyone else is happy.

Graduation day is so much more than just a ceremony where you hear speeches about the future and receive your diploma. Graduation day is a symbolic transition in life. It is a rite of passage, signifying that you have made it successfully though childhood and are ready for the next stage of life. Graduation day is also about celebrating the fact that you have overcome all the obstacles and roadblocks life has put in your path. In other words, every human being encounters some problems at home, with friends, or at school. Making it to graduation day shows everyone, including yourself, that you succeeded despite those problems.

Graduation is the time to reflect on all of the people who have helped you succeed in life. For some of you, this might be your parents, grandparents, older brother or sister, or other family members. For others it might be close friends. It may even be someone like a church leader, a coach, Boy Scout or Girl Scout troop leader, or maybe a club or activity sponsor. Trust us, these people, that is, the people who have supported you through the good times and the bad times will be just as excited for you as anyone else. In fact, as principals, we often say that graduation day is as much for the parents, families, and other adults as it is for the graduates. Everyone feels a great sense of accomplishment.

What will *your* graduation day be like? It may seem far away, but from our viewpoints as high school educators who have worked with students just like you for many years, believe us when we tell you that your graduation day will be here before you know it. How proud will your family be of you on graduation day? How proud will you be of yourself?

Andres Rodriguez

Graduation day is closer than you think! Today is the day you start to set yourself up for not only a great high school experience... but a great life!

WHY YOU SHOULD LISTEN TO WHAT WE SAY

As two adults who have worked exclusively with high school students for almost 40 years combined, we have much experience in what it takes to be successful in high school. We have been teachers (of every grade level, but mostly of ninth graders), coaches, club sponsors, school administrators, and, finally, principals. We have seen how savvy students manage high school like experts. These students were able to get good grades, be involved in activities that interested them, made great relationships, and had fun. We have taken all the positive actions and ideas of these students and put them in this book for you. That's right; you are going to have an advantage over some of your peers because you are going to have ***insider's knowledge*** from some of the most successful students.

Think about this concept for a second. If you could go back and redo your middle school years, would you do anything differently? We bet you would. If we asked you to give some hints to rising sixth graders to help them be more successful in middle school, could you do it? Some of your hints might have to do with academics, and some of the others probably concern activities. Some of your hints might relate to dealing with friends or social interactions. You probably remember thinking that some things seemed so important at eleven or twelve years old, and now you realize these things are not important at all. Also, we bet the opposite is true. We are sure that there are some things you wished you had taken more seriously or done in a better way. If you could give this advice now to kids entering middle school next year, it would be valuable to them because you have *experience*. In other words, you have lived through middle school, have perspective on what is important and what is not important, and have survived.

Basically, we are offering you this type of advice as you get ready for high school. The students with whom we have worked over the years are now going to pass on their advice through us to help you have a better high school experience. Here is an example of what we mean. Each year in the spring of our students' senior year, we ask our soon-to-be graduates one thing they wish they could have done differently in high school. Almost every student says they wished they had taken their freshman year classes and grades more seriously. Many of them bemoan the fact that they didn't understand what a grade point average was, or how their freshman year classes impacted their grade point averages. Many of them talk about having had to "repair" their grades or scramble during their junior year so their grade point averages would be competitive enough to apply to the colleges of their choice. These types of insights, and the specifics of how to implement these ideas, are what you will find throughout this book.

Our goal is not only to help you get to graduation day, but also to help you thrive in high school. If this goal comes true, you will be academically prepared for the next stage of your life. You will have had great experiences and memories from high school, and you will have made some lifelong friends.

Chapter One

This May Be the Most Important Book You Will Ever Read

Students' experiences in their first year of high school often determine their success throughout high school and beyond. However, more students fail ninth grade than any other grade." —Williams & Richman, 2007

So you are headed to high school next year. You are probably thinking, "What's the big deal? It is just another year of school, right?" Wrong. The ninth grade year is the most important year of your education. People who do nothing else but study our nation's schools have even given ninth grade a special name; they call it the "make-it or break-it" year. School leaders all over the country are working hard to help students experience success in this first year of high school. Some school districts have built expensive special school buildings just for ninth graders. Other large schools have broken themselves into several smaller ninth grade "academies" to make the high school experience more personalized in their efforts to improve student success rates. Virtually every high school has implemented some kind of freshman transition program designed to smooth the journey from middle to high school. These programs are often very time-consuming and expensive. It makes you wonder why this one year of schooling gets so much attention, doesn't it? Good news! We are going to tell you why such a fuss is being made.

TWO THINGS THAT YOU NEED TO KNOW ABOUT THE FRESHMAN YEAR

It is important that we prove to you that success in the freshman year is important in setting yourself up not only for a great high school career, but also for a happy and successful life. Also, we promise you that your high school experience will not resemble what is portrayed in the movies or on TV in the least. Let's start with what you need to know about the freshman year.

Success Leads to More Success

There are quite a few researchers who study why students experience success in school. They do this research in the hopes of identifying certain factors that successful students tend to have in common. They believe that once these factors are identified, they can attempt to replicate them in the school experience of all students. This, in turn, would hopefully lead to more and more students succeeding in high school.

These researchers look at huge piles of data and student records searching for things called "predictors." A "predictor" is a factor that, when tested in statistical formulas, is good at forecasting future events. For example, research has proven that smoking cigarettes is a predictor of having a greater chance of getting cancer. Or, research has proven that getting regular exercise increases a person's chances of living longer.

Many researchers and statisticians have zeroed in on one predictor that, more than any other, will indicate success in high school and beyond: the ninth grade year. They have found, time and again, that students who get off to a good start in high school are likely to maintain that momentum throughout their entire high school careers. It is almost as if, once a student gets that taste of success, he or she craves it and does not let anything get in the way of continuing to succeed. In fact, if you form good habits during your freshman year, the rest of your high school career will feel easier as a result.

Failure Leads to More Failure

Unfortunately for many students across our country, this same research described above says that the opposite is also true. In fact, researchers have found that students who have fallen behind their

Lorraine Swanson

Successful high school students often set themselves up for success by forming study groups early in their ninth grade year.

peers by the end of their ninth grade year are twenty times more likely to drop out of high school before earning their diplomas. Twenty times! This statistic is very scary to a lot of people. It scares school district leaders, principals, teachers, parents, and, most importantly, it probably scares you as a rising high school student. We don't want you to be scared, however. We want you to find out how you can set yourself up for success in the ninth grade, and we have more good news for you: This book is going to give you the knowledge you need to make that happen.

WHY IS THE NINTH GRADE SO IMPORTANT?

You might be asking, "Why is the ninth grade year so important?" This is a valid question for you to have. Of all the years of schooling, what makes this one year in particular stand out as so much more important than the others? The fact is that this year is the first time your performance in school really counts. Please don't confuse counts with matters. All of your schooling matters! The education you have received in your elementary and middle school years is foundational and important to your future success in high school. The key difference in ninth grade is that your performance, from the very first day of your ninth grade year until you have completed your graduation requirements, is tracked and recorded. Some of you may have actually started on your high school record already if you have taken or are taking high school credit courses, such as Algebra I or Spanish. Make sure to know if these courses will go on your permanent high school transcript, as your school district may allow your parents/guardians to expunge the eighth grade courses from your record.

As you start high school, your grades will begin to build a formal record of your academic progress. High schools call this record your "transcript." Any institution that you want to be considered for after high school, whether it is a vocational training center, a top college or university, or future employers, will look closely at your transcript when deciding whether to offer you a spot for admission or a job. The grades you earn in your ninth grade year count every bit as much as the ones you will earn in your other three years of high school. These grades are all averaged together to create your cumulative grade point average (GPA). Your GPA is an extremely important factor in the college admissions process. The GPA is also important in deciding things like scholarships (worth as much as hundreds and thousands of dollars for your family) and eligibility to become a member of clubs, such as the National Honor Society. Additionally, colleges and universities use your GPA when making selections to prestigious summer programs and internship opportunities during high school that are held at their schools.

Although your GPA is very important, we don't want to forget to impress upon you just how important the material you will be covering in your ninth grade classes will be for your future learning experiences. The topics and ideas that you will be learning in your freshman classes (algebra, geometry, world history, physical science, biology, literature, etc.) consist of vitally important academic knowledge. They will be heavily weighted on the college entrance examinations (SAT and ACT) that you will be taking in your eleventh and twelfth grade years. Often they are the foundation for many of the courses you will take later in high school.

Insider's Tip: Good grades are important, and will largely be what college admissions will be based on, but LEARNING is what school is really all about. Embrace the knowledge that you are being given access to, not just the grades that you receive from your teachers.

So now you know that ninth grade is important, and the research has shown you that a solid ninth grade year is an important factor in having an overall successful high school career. All that's left for us is to do is to convince you that it is in your own best interests to have a great high school career. For that, we have two factors we would like you to consider.

Money

People who do well in high school make more money. That is a fact. We're sure that you are saying, "I've heard of people who were high school dropouts who became rich and famous." That statement is true; those people exist. But those are "one-in-a-million" cases. By far, the most common scenario is:

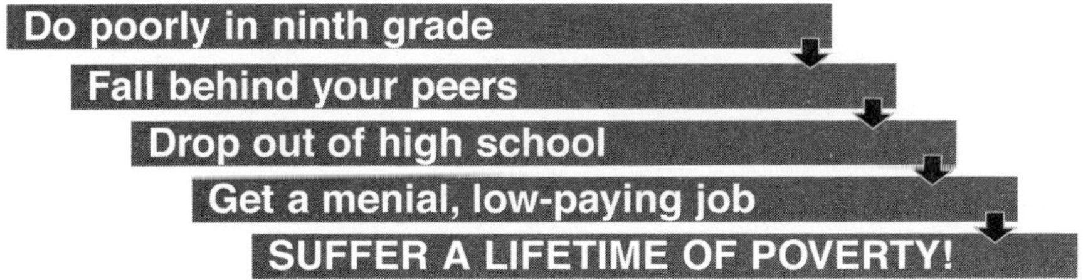

There is good research to back up this scenario. In 2005, the average high school dropout was paid $17,299 per year. The average person with a high school diploma, but no additional training or education, earned $26,933. Workers who continued their education after high school and completed an Associate's Degree (earned from a two-year college) made an average of $36,645. Those who attended a four-year college or university and earned their Bachelor's Degrees earned an average of $52,671.

Therefore, the difference in earnings between a person who dropped out of high school and one who completed high school and went on to successfully graduate from a four-year college or university was $35,372 per year. Multiply that difference by a lifetime of work (40 years), and that number grows to $1,414,880! That huge amount of money represents what the college graduate's lifetime earnings are over that of a high school dropout. Okay, okay. We can hear it now. You're thinking, "Money isn't everything." We have an answer for that, too!

Happiness

There have been studies that have connected people's "Quality of Life Index" with the amount of schooling they have completed. The "Quality of Life Index" is the general feeling of "happiness" or "satisfaction" with one's life. Guess what? Research shows that the more schooling a person has, the happier they tend to be. There are many reasons for people claiming that they are "happy" or "very happy," but some of the most common are:

- **Being surrounded by family and friends**
- **Having the ability to give back to society**
- **Having meaningful work that is valued by self and others**
- **Feeling a sense of freedom in one's life**

It is safe to say that many of these factors can be positively impacted by educational success. A college degree doesn't guarantee that you will be surrounded by family and friends, but it certainly could help you have the resources and the ability to give back to society. It is likely to allow you to have a greater feeling of the worth of the work you choose to do in your life. It will probably provide you with the opportunity to have a greater sense of freedom and control over your own destiny; and, finally, it will improve your chances of feeling that you have succeeded both personally and professionally.

So if you want to be rich, happy, and successful, make sure that you have a great high school career. We know the secrets to how many high school students have succeeded in the past, and we are going to share them with you in this book. We will give you tips on how to plan for success in your high school career, teach you how to organize yourself in ways that promote good habits, show you how to get involved in the right activities that will support your development as a person and student, give you the secrets to developing great relationships with all the important people in your lives, show you how to work with your parents to establish the rules you need to follow over your teen years, and show you how to keep track of your progress in your classes.

Through all of these tips and methods, you will find that success in high school is as easy as 1, 2, 3. We're not going to promise that it won't be hard work, but you'll know you are headed in the right direction. It won't take long for you to begin to see the results. Trust us!

Chapter Two

The Importance of a Good Plan

If you don't know where you're going, the chances are you'll end up somewhere else. —Yogi Berra

For the sake of argument, let's compare your high school journey to how you might help plan your family's summer vacation. A summer vacation is an important and expensive event for your family, so you won't want to leave anything to chance. First, you sit down with your parents to decide where you want go for this vacation. Will it be a week at the beach? Will you travel to Disney World? Maybe you'll plan a trip to a national park, such as the Grand Canyon. During this meeting, you and your family develop a vision for your summer vacation, calculating whether the options you describe are realistic and within budget. Developing a clear idea of where you are going is the most important part of the planning process. If you don't have a destination in mind, you will be wandering around aimlessly and, frankly, you will waste your family's summer break getting not much done. First, your family must settle on a destination for a summer getaway. Once you know where you want to go, you are ready to take the next step.

Many hours of planning will be necessary for this vacation to become a reality. You need to have a clear idea of how you will get to your vacation spot. Will you be flying or driving? Let's say you decide to drive. Someone will have to do the necessary research to plot the course by using a roadmap or getting directions from Google® maps. You will want to make sure that you have some back-up contacts, like roadside assistance, that can help put you back on track in case something goes wrong on the road. As you know, things rarely go perfectly as planned, so you will want to remain flexible in case something comes up that makes you alter the route during the trip. All of these preparations will be important to guiding you to your destination smoothly.

If you take these steps, you have greatly increased the chances that your vacation will be both successful and enjoyable. Such planning and preparation are equally important to success in both vacations, such as the one we just imagined, and for your high school career. You must know where you want to end up right from the moment you begin your high school career. You need to research how to prepare to put yourself in the best position to reach your future goals. You must also develop a set of resources that are in place to help you reach your destination. In this chapter we will explain how you should plan with your parents or guardians for the next four years so that, when you high school career is completed, you will be in position to reach your goals for your post-secondary life.

Mary Symons

High school can be a confusing place for students who don't know where they are going!

DEVELOPING A VISION

Do you have a vision for where you will be in four years? Will you be entering the workforce as a recent high school graduate? Will you be heading off to a university or a community college? Will you be preparing to enter the armed forces to begin your career in the military? If you don't have any ideas about how to answer these types of questions, you are just like the vast majority of rising ninth graders we've worked with over our years as high school educators. Yet, the fact that high school freshmen so often head into this really important stage of their educations with such little planning never ceases to amaze us! As we've said earlier, the ninth grade year is perhaps the most important year of all. Anything is possible for a new ninth grader; all the "doors of opportunity" are open at this time. It is during the freshmen year, however, when many students see "doors begin to close" as a result of poor planning and poor understanding of what it takes to be successful in high school. Are you ready to begin reducing the options in your life at your age? We want the opposite to be true. When you are young, you should have many options and opportunities open to you as you grow to become an adult.

We encourage rising ninth graders to engage in rich and open conversations with their parents or guardians when they are developing their vision for their high school careers. These discussions can even be fun! Perhaps for the first time ever, you will have real adult conversations with those people who love and care for you the most about what and where you want to be when you finish school. We think that it is important for you to be honest about your dreams for the future, but not in a childish or immature way. If your dream is to be a professional baseball player, a famous recording artist, or an attendee at a prestigious school like Harvard University, we encourage you to embrace those dreams! For some students, these dreams are possible. Planning in a mature way, however, you need to find out what it takes for these dreams to become reality. The chances are good, however, that if your dreams are truly

Table 1. Insider's Edge Vision Inventory

Rising Ninth Grade Student	***Parent(s)***
What are your dreams for the future for the future? (Reach for the stars!)	*What are your dreams for the your teen? (Reach for the stars!)*
What do you think it will take for you to achieve these dreams?	*What do you think it will take for your teen to achieve these dreams?*
What is your "back-up plan" for your future?	*What is a great "back-up plan" for your teen?*
What will it take to achieve this "back-up plan"?	*What will it take for your teen to achieve this "back-up plan"?*

"out of this world," you may not achieve them. This is why it is also important for you to begin to develop a solid "back-up plan" for what you might want to do if your dream scenario does not become a reality.

We believe that all students getting ready to enter high school should have a meaningful conversation about their dreams and plans with their parents or guardians. We realize that having this conversation can be difficult and not so much fun for you. That's why we have developed our "vision inventory" (Table 1). This tool will help you develop a vision and will guide you as you sit down with your family to discuss your goals. We know you are thinking that you don't want to have this conversation, but you have to. It won't be as painful as you think, and it will help you out tremendously with your parents. While you are developing this vision inventory, be open to your parents' ideas and feelings about your future. Remember that nothing you do here is written in stone. These are just discussions to start the planning process for your high school career. Complete the vision inventory in Table 1 now.

NOW, DO YOUR HOMEWORK!

Now that you have developed a vision for what you want out of your high school career, it is important for you to begin to do the research to create an "action plan" that will help guide you as you begin. Before creating such a plan, you have some homework to do! You can research the careers you are interested in on the internet, you can contact your school's college/career counselor, and you can begin networking with people in the fields in which you are interested to find out what further schooling or training one would need to enter this occupation successfully. Are their special skills or experiences that would help smooth your way into this field? What are the best schools or training programs available for preparation? What will it take to be admitted to these schools or programs? Any time you spend on this can be considered time well spent because it is all about your future. Remember, there are sometimes other high schools nearby that offer

Table 2. Insider's Edge Post-Secondary Plan

POST-SECONDARY PLAN	
Primary Ambitions	***Realistic "Back-Up" Plan***
State your chosen plan:	*State your chosen back-up plan:*
What level of education, training, preparation, and other factors will you need to achieve this goal? *Education:* *Training:* *Preparation:* *Other factors:*	*What level of education, training, preparation, and other factors will you need to achieve this goal?* *Education:* *Training:* *Preparation:* *Other factors:*
Describe what type of high school achievement will likely be necessary for you to realize this ambition:	*Describe what type of high school achievement will likely be necessary for you to realize this ambition:*
What other activities will increase your chances of realizing this goal?	*What other activities will increase your chances of realizing this goal?*

certain academic or specialty programs that may be of interest to you. There may be an "international studies program" or a course of study focused on "bio-tech engineering." You need to know which schools around you offer Advanced Placement courses in the academic area of special interest to you. There may even be schools where students can earn special diplomas such as International Baccalaureate or Cambridge Programme certificates upon graduation. All of this kind of research will help you find out which high school is the best fit for you.

NOW MAKE THE PLAN

Now that you've done your research, it is time to sit down with your parents or guardians to complete the more formal "Post-Secondary Plan" located in Table 2. Remember that this is just an initial plan to help guide you as you start your high school career. It should be a "living document" that is revisited often as your plans for the future change as you mature. Simply completing this document, however, is a big step toward heading in the right direction for a great high school career and life!

Chapter Three

Get Yourself Organized

The secret of all victory lies in the organization of the non-obvious.
—Emperor Marcus Aurelius

We have worked with thousands of successful students and have noticed that many of these students share some common qualities and characteristics that have helped them achieve that success. One of these characteristics is their ability to organize to allow them to manage their busy lives in high school in a seemingly effortless way. These students always seem to know exactly what they have done, what they are doing, and what they need to do next. Many of them use the same or similar tools to make sure they are always on top of their games. We have identified four tools we think are most important to use to experience success in high school.

PROTOCOLS AND PROCEDURES FOR SUCCESS

We use the term, "protocols and procedures," to describe the methods and steps many of our best students use to organize themselves, thereby putting themselves on track to experience success in high school. We know that this discussion sounds boring and lame, but we have to tell you that if you clearly develop an organizational system, understand it, and put it into place before school starts, you will have a much greater opportunity to experience success as a high school student. We have heard time and again how other students hate how the successful students make it look "so easy" to get good grades and be successful in school. In reality, it is not easy at all! It is simply that most good students have organizational systems in place that allow them to get things done and get them done well without looking like they are stressed or overwhelmed. We encourage you to work with your parents or guardians to develop your system for success. Remember, often they have had to face and overcome many of the same organizational issues you will face in high school. They can be a great resource.

Tool #1 - Use a Daily Planner

Many schools provide every student with a daily planner at the beginning of each school year. Most of these daily planners are custom-made for the school and include items, such as maps, school calendars, student handbooks, and other important information. If your school does not provide a daily planner to you, ask your parents to purchase one for you. This tool will become one of the best investments of your life! It never ceases to amaze us that so few high school students use daily planners to keep themselves organized. As adults, we couldn't imagine living without one.

Your life is about to get much, much more complicated. The life of the average high school student is unbelievably hectic and busy. We wonder how students manage to fit everything they are asked to do into their schedules. Some students, however, seem to be able to do everything they are asked and still have time to enjoy a healthy, happy social life. How do they manage this? Usually these students are disciplined and committed users of their daily planner.

Students who use their planners regularly tend to fall into two general categories. The first group is made up of those students who are naturally organized and wouldn't consider going through a class, much less an entire school day, without a planner. If you are one of these types of students, we offer you our sincere congratulations. The rest of this section may just be a review for you. If you are still reading, you are both normal and just like both of the authors of this book. You will need to be trained and prodded into using a daily planner until it becomes a normal practice in your life.

To get started, work with your parents to establish some protocols and procedures about how you will use your daily planner to stay on top of what you are expected to do in high school. These rules will help keep you honest and routine in the use of your planner. We have asked some of our most successful students what their rules for daily planner use are and have compiled a list. Some of the practices you may want to consider include the following:

- Write down the daily assignment for each class in the planner every time the class meets. This practice is important for consistency and serves as a good reference if the teacher reports missing work later.
- Write down important due dates for long-term class assignments in the planner as soon as they are announced. Be sure to include several "checkpoint" dates in the planner, usually halfway between the day the project was assigned and the due date and another two or three days prior to the due date. This practice helps you avoid procrastination, which is a common pitfall for high school students.
- Keep track of important meetings of clubs, sporting events, concerts, activities, and any other activities that require you to spend afternoon, evening, or weekend time at school or at a school event. This practice is also helpful for your parents since they will quite often need to coordinate their schedules with these events so they can attend as well. (See Chapter 4: "You Need to Be Involved.") Finally, the daily planner is the place for you to keep track of your personal appointments, friends and study partners' phone numbers and email addresses, birthdays, and social events, etc.

Many people are using "smart phones" or other electronic devices to take the place of all paper and pencil daily planners. We caution students about relying on this type of technology because many district and school rules continue to prohibit students from using electronics during the school day. Should school rules change to allow you to use these technologies, "daily planner" should be used as a universal term for any mechanism one can use to keep track of your busy schedule.

Your parents may want to establish a routine at the beginning of the school year to check your planner every day. We know that this

Alex Carter

Maintaining a daily planner is the key to many successful students' life.

sounds annoying and childlike, but we want to encourage you to go along with this practice. This way you will have the added support and external motivation to get everything done on time. Plus, this is a good way for you to keep you parents or guardians informed about what you are doing in your school life. If you find this practice too distasteful, make a deal with your parents or guardians to "suspend" this practice once you have demonstrated that you are staying on top of your work. A good time to talk about "suspending" would be at the end of the first grading period where, because of your excellent organizational skills, you will have earned good grades and comments from all your teachers.

The bottom line is that maintaining the daily planner regularly and completely will make your life as a high school student much more manageable and enjoyable. It will also establish a lifelong organizational habit that will benefit you in college and beyond.

Tool #2 - Develop Rules for When and How Work Will Be Done at Home

Most high school students we have worked with value their privacy and independence, which is a good and normal thing for students who are developing into adults! This doesn't mean, however, that your parents or guardians, who have spent the last 14 years guiding you and helping you grow up, are all of a sudden going to give up all of their influence over when, where, and how you will do your schoolwork.

What is important is that you are now a "partner" in developing the rules for completing your schoolwork at home. You can choose to use this discussion as a method to show your parents or guardians how mature and collaborative you are becoming. How well you manage this conversation can be a way for you to gain greater independence and control later in your high school career. However this conversation goes, we highly recommend that you develop some protocols and procedures for how you will get your work done at home. In our work with countless successful students, we have noticed that most of them have simple and straightforward rules they follow to make sure they are always ready and prepared for classes. These rules include:

Homework is done at the same time every day

Homework is done in a clean, quiet workspace away from outside interruptions

Use parents/guardians to review major assignments for proofreading and edits

These simple rules help successful students focus only on the work. With these rules in place, life becomes less complicated. They no longer have to worry about when or how the work will be done. Many of these students rely on their parents to check and ensure that all schoolwork has been completed in a timely and organized fashion. These rules actually improve, rather than worsen, the relationship between these students and their parents/guardians. We really encourage you to work with your parents to develop these rules before you enter your freshman year and before things get complicated. You'll be thankful later on.

Tool #3 – Know Exactly What Is Expected of You

One of the major stumbling blocks for ninth graders is the different expectations of each teacher. Although some schools are trying to have teachers work more cooperatively together to align their classroom expectations, the reality is that many teachers still have unique and different norms in their classroom, including how to format assignments when they are handed in, policies for accepting late work, and allowances to redo tests or assignments that are not up to expectations. These are just examples of policies that might be different in each class you have at high school.

Over the years the most successful students we work with are rarely confused or unsure about what their teachers, coaches, or club sponsors expect from them. They make sure they have a clear understanding of what they need to do to succeed on the current assignment. How do they always know? If they are unsure, they ask! Because they have written themselves reminder notes and checkpoint dates in their daily planner, they have many opportunities to evaluate their understanding of the assignment or project they have been asked to complete. If they discover they are confused or unsure about the direction they are heading, they make certain to schedule an appointment with the teacher to review and clarify what they are being required to do. These students never leave an important assignment to the last minute. Therefore, they are sure they know what they need to do, have a good idea of how much time it will take, and know what materials or outside resources they will need to create a quality product. Their preplanning and organization have once again put them in a position of success. Learn from these students!

Tool #4 – Good Time Management

Our most successful students seem to be extremely busy, but they rarely appear to be overwhelmed or time-crunched. How can this be? We have noticed that these students are highly aware of what they need to be doing and manage their time very effectively. They create "to do" lists and refer to them often during the day. Also, they will prioritize their "to do" lists so they are sure to complete the most important and time-sensitive items on the list first. They ensure that they get the essential tasks completed before they run out of time. (Yes, these students run out of time too.) Also, they always are sure to do the item that is due first thing tomorrow. We have also noticed that the most successful students are experts at using "down time" in school productively. Instead of daydreaming during those extra "free" minutes that sometimes are provided at the end of a class, these students are getting something done. This way they have time to do things they want to do later in the day. Don't think that these students are always working and never have fun! They actually have *more* fun because there is no guilt factor when they are goofing around. They already have everything they need to do in complete shape for tomorrow. They aren't worried about what happens later.

We hope that you think about how you can adopt some of these organizational strategies and habits that some of our most successful students use to keep on top of their school lives. We know that if you stick with them, you will find that high school success will be yours to enjoy.

Chapter Four

You Need to Be Involved

So, you might be thinking…the previous two chapters were helpful and important, but when does the fun start? You know, the stuff you've been hearing about from your friends' older brothers and sisters, including all the excitement that goes along with high school. These are the fun high school activities everyone talks about, like homecoming, pep rallies, dances, football games, plays, musicals, concerts, prom, and so much more. You've probably heard stories about high school teachers, or how hard some of the classes are and that has you worried, but all the other things that go on outside the classroom are why you are really looking forward to the next four years of your life. We encourage you to embrace these outside-the-classroom experiences. They are what make high school an exciting and memorable experience!

THE NEXT FOUR YEARS WILL BE THE BEST YEARS OF YOUR LIFE (SO FAR)

After watching thousands of teenagers navigate high school, we can clearly tell you that the ones who got the most out of high school are the ones who got involved in their school beyond the walls of the classroom. When we say, "Get the most out of high school," we mean that they made lifelong friends and made memories they will never forget. In fact, when you ask most graduating seniors to describe their favorite memory from high school, most of them will describe a club, a sport, or an activity they were involved with in school or outside the regular school day.

In addition to making lifelong friends and memories, when we say, "Get the most out of high school," that is, getting involved in activities, clubs, or sports, we also mean that you will become a well-round-

Jose Gill

The friendships you make in your extracurricular activities can last a lifetime.

ed person. These experiences help you develop skills and confidence, meet new people, and learn more about life than just what you will learn from your teachers in the classroom.

Getting involved in an activity, club, or sport enables you to make a connection to your school in addition to just going to class each day. This connection helps you develop a school spirit or loyalty for your high school. It gives you a larger purpose than just attending school each day; rather, this connection is a reason to get the most out of each day. These connections are also important because, we're here to tell you, you will have some rough days ahead. Not every day will go well in high school. There are all sorts of pitfalls that happen to a teenager. The connections you make by being involved in school activities will become the support system that will help you get through those rough days.

ARE YOU BEING HONEST WITH YOURSELF?

How are you feeling about going to high school next year? Be honest. If you are like 99% of other teenagers getting ready to attend high school, you are experiencing a mixture of emotions. You're "done" with middle school (the rules, the immaturity of the younger students, etc.), so you are most likely really excited to start this new part of your life. When you see high school students they look grown up, independent. Their lives seem like so much fun. At the same time, you most likely are very nervous and anxious. Some of the students look very grown up and scary. The building is much bigger than your school now. You might have heard that some of the teachers are mean and the classes are hard. Probably of most importance is that you're not sure where you'll fit in. What will your identity be at the school? Will the other kids be nice to you? If you're being honest with yourself, it feels a bit overwhelming just thinking about it all.

We remember one student (maybe just like you), who was very nervous about coming to high school. In fact, his mother was just as overwhelmed. They couldn't believe that he was about to go to high school with all those "big" kids and those "old" looking teenagers.

He ended up transitioning to high school easily with no problems. In fact, he thrived in his transition. He did well academically, he made new friends, he was able to navigate the school with no problems, and he fit in. Do you want to know his secret? He got involved in an activity that actually began a few weeks before the school year began – the school's marching band.

The most important part of this success story is that he wasn't successful because the band was really good or because it's beneficial to play a musical instrument (which it is), but rather because of the connections he made with the people involved with the marching band. He made friends; he had an identity. He belonged! Isn't that what it's all about for you right now? You want to make sure you *belong* at your new school. Of course, some practical side benefits are also associated with getting involved in an activity so early in the school year. For example, he made friends with some upper classmen who he knew could answer his questions. He had someone to sit with at lunch the first day (always a traumatic episode for new ninth graders). If he got lost in the school, he had a network of friends who looked out for him and helped him find his way.

Insider's Tip: If you can find a way to get involved in a sport, club, or activity before school starts, there are huge benefits to making friends, getting comfortable, and knowing the school even before the first day of classes.

HOW DO I GET INVOLVED AT MY HIGH SCHOOL

Where you live and the size of your high school might determine the amount of clubs, activities, and sports that are available to you as a student. During the spring of your eighth grade year you should begin researching what is available at the high school you will attend. First, explore the school's website to see what is available. Write down some possibilities that interest you and other basic information. Keep in mind that some schools have better websites than others; therefore, you might not get a true picture of everything that is available at the school.

Next, you should begin asking around about the different clubs, activities, and sports. Often you can gather really valuable information from students who are already attending the school. For example, is there a student you trust who attended your middle school and is now is in the high school? Those students might be able to give you some "inside" information about the best clubs to get involved with at the school.

Which Activity Should I Get Involved In?

The correct answer to this question is that as long as you get involved in any activity you will be doing the right thing. In fact, you might be shocked to learn how many students never get involved in anything, so just by getting involved in something you will be helping yourself to a better high school experience than many other students. That being said, here are a few hints for finding the right activity or club.

What Are Your Interests?

A simple answer to the question about which club/activity to get involved with is to find one related to your interests. There has never been a better time to go to high school. One advantage you will have that maybe your parents didn't have is that high schools have made tremendous efforts to offer a huge variety of clubs and activities in an attempt to attract students no matter what their interests are.

What Are Your Friends Doing?

Sometimes finding out what some of your closest friends are interested in can help you find the right club. If you are not sure of what club to join, maybe you could convince a friend or two to join a club with you. In this way you'll have the security of a friend and a better comfort level as you begin to meet other students in that club.

Find a School Spirited Activity

Joining activities such as the homecoming committee or the Student Government are great ways to begin to be a part of the school and take part in fun activities. The adults and students in charge of these activities are always looking for extra help and almost always have things for extra volunteers to do. Even if you don't want to run for a class office position or do not get elected, there are tons of ways to be involved in Student Government. In fact, many students who have the most fun in Student Government are not the actual students who were elected.

Many Clubs Are Service Oriented

Some clubs may have titles that don't really explain what the club does or participates in, but have really worthy missions. In other words, if you see a club with a title like the Key Club, you may not realize the important service-oriented work or community benefit this club provides. Many students

Insider's Tip: In the first two weeks of school, find out who the Student Government sponsor (teacher) is and go see him or her. Ask that teacher how you (and your friends if you want) can get involved with planning and preparing for homecoming activities. This strategic move on your part will immediately create a connection with the sponsor, help you meet new friends, and get you involved with the excitement of homecoming and the beginning of the school year.

find these clubs to be the most rewarding. Not only will you make a huge difference in the lives of some people who might need it, but also you'll make friends as you work together for a positive purpose. A side benefit of service-oriented clubs is that participation in these clubs (or better yet, leadership positions) look great on college applications.

Activities Outside of School

Activities outside of school are also positive. While they may not necessarily be directly related to your transition to high school, some of the most successful students we have seen are ones who are involved with Boy Scouts or Girl Scouts of America or with their religious/ church youth groups.

These activities can also be highly regarded by colleges/universities. If you find other great non-school-related activities, we encourage you to also become a part of those.

What If There Is No Activity at School for Me?

Do you know that the average person's taste buds, what they like to eat or drink, change every seven years? That's why foods you might have hated as a child you might love today. The opposite can also be true: foods that you loved as a child might not appeal to you anymore. This change in food tastes, for the average person, will continue as they get older.

The same can be said about your interests and hobbies. As you are getting older, different things will appeal to you. Think about it. You might have loved the "Teletubbies" or "Bob the Builder" when you were a toddler, but you don't watch those shows anymore. As you got a little bit older, you started watching Hannah Montana or the Jonas Brothers. Will you still be watching these shows in a few years? Probably not. The point is that as we get older our tastes and interests change. Don't be so quick to judge that there is no club or activity for you. In some ways, the beginning of high school is a new chapter in your life. Don't be afraid to try out clubs and activities that wouldn't have interested you in sixth or seventh grade. You're not in sixth or seventh grade anymore. You're going to high school. Your best memories await you. Don't close you mind because you think something might not interest you.

Can We Start Our Own Club?

If you are still not convinced that there is a club or activity for you at your high school, you can explore the idea of starting your own club. The process of starting a new club is going to be different at each school, so we can only give you some generic recommendations. As a rising ninth grader, however, there are some real benefits to considering this idea. First, once that club is established, you'll be able to enjoy it and participate in it for all four years of high school. Second, starting your own club as a freshman, becoming a leader, and sustaining that club through all four years is extremely impressive and will look amazing on your college applications.

That being said, starting your own club may prove to be tricky. First, your school district most likely has rules (usually called a "regulation") about how to start your own club. Sometimes clubs can be school-sponsored, or they might allow you to have an "Equal Access" club. "Equal Access" was created so no one group or organization could be denied the right to meet when other groups are allowed to meet. Sometimes approval for new clubs is left up to the principal; sometimes approval must come from the School Board. We recommend that you first get the support of your parents because you might need their help with this project. Next, seek out a faculty member who will agree to sponsor your new club or organization. Having this person on board and in place before you request administrative approval greatly increases the odds of receiving permission for your new club to form.

HOW DO I BECOME WELL ROUNDED?

The term, *well-rounded,* simply means that you are able to show that you are not just totally focused in one area. For example, drama and acting may have become a passion of yours. You have been in plays since you were a little kid. You have taken acting classes, and your parents have sent you to acting camp, etc. So you know that, when you enter high school, you're surely going to get involved in the drama program. This is a positive decision. However, make sure that you find something else, something away from drama, to also get involved in. Your level of involvement doesn't have to be at the same commitment, and you certainly don't have to devote the same amount of time to this side activity, but it is healthy to have other interests as well.

This same issue can happen in sports. Some students devote themselves to their sport year round. For example, there are many year-round swimmers, who devote hours and hours to practicing, going to meets on weekends, etc. They know for sure that they want to be on their high school swim team. We love this dedication to a healthy life- long sport! Plus, we love the fact that these athletes want to represent their schools in competitive interscholastic swimming. However, we also believe that these students should find something else in which to be involved. A variety of interests makes you a well-rounded person.

Again, don't expect that you can devote the same amount of dedication and time to everything. You must make choices about how to balance different activities and be truly dedicated to the things you love the most.

DON'T OVEREXTEND YOURSELF

The purpose of finding a club, activity, or sport in which to get involved is to help make friends, ease your transition to high school, do something you like, and have fun. The purpose is not to get involved with every activity at your school. We have seen students make this critical mistake, thinking that they want to do everything, or that somehow this will make them more appealing to colleges. What happens is that these students' grades begin to suffer, or they get so stressed out trying to keep up with their schoolwork and all their other responsibilities, that it defeats the purpose of getting involved with these activities.

While it is true that colleges will want you to be a well-rounded student and will look at your involvement in sports, clubs, and activities as positive factors, they are not looking for students who have joined many clubs simply to have a long impressive list of memberships. Most colleges are looking first for academically focused students. (Remember that your grades must always be your first priority.) Next, colleges are looking for students who are involved in a few quality experiences in clubs, activities, and sports. Leadership positions are a huge advantage, so try to put yourself in a position during your ninth grade year to learn from the upperclassmen leaders so that in a couple of years you could be in a leadership role.

"I REALLY WANT TO PLAY SPORTS AT MY HIGH SCHOOL"

Generally speaking, high school athletics can be highly competitive. Usually, your skill as an athlete and your experience in the sport will determine if you will be able to "make the team," and earn playing time in games. Keep in mind that being involved with the sporting team is likely to be a valuable and rewarding experience no matter how much playing time you might earn. Being involved with your school and its sports teams will give you a sense of belonging, gives you a chance to make new friends, allows you to represent your school, and gives you experience in being part of a team. Don't lose perspective on the purpose of your involvement.

We know a young lady who was highly involved with her school's lacrosse team. This team did very well finishing the regular season with an undefeated record, winning the district championship, the regional championship, and going to the state tournament. This athlete, who happened to be a senior, didn't get very much playing time. In fact, as the games got more important and against tougher competition, she didn't play at all. The amazing part of this story is that even though she didn't play in the games much, it didn't bother her a bit. She was happy to be part of the success, part of the team, and enjoy being around her friends.

When we asked her about how she dealt with the fact that she didn't get much playing time, she showed great perspective. "I have had the time of life being a part of this team. Some of the other girls are better than me, so I understand why they play more. My best friends are on this team with me and I will never forget this season."

We can't explain it any better. Don't misinterpret what we are saying. We want you to work hard, practice hard, try to play in games, and be a positive contributor to your athletic team. But don't lose perspective on the real reason you should be involved with athletics at your high school. The real reason to be involved in sports is to have fun, learn new skills, make friends, and form positive life-long memories.

How Do I Get Started?

First, most states have a requirement that you get a physical examination by a physician clearing you for participation in athletic activity before you will be allowed to try out for any sport. Make sure you find out about any requirement like this and have your parents assist you with filling out the right forms well before the first day of tryouts. We have seen many students miss the first few days of tryouts because the right forms were not completed and turned in on time. These actions will put you at a disadvantage to the other players who did everything correctly, so make sure to take care of these requirements ahead of time.

Next, many sports actually start with workouts or conditioning before the first official day of practice. Research your school's website to find this information. If you cannot find out the information you want on the school's website, call the school or make contact with the coach to find out. Note that, if you plan to participate in a fall sport or activity (like marching band, football, cross country, field hockey, soccer, etc.), these usually start a few weeks before the first day of school, and you don't want to miss several weeks of practice, which would be a severe disadvantage.

Tryouts

Most schools and sports teams are required to give athletes a certain number of days to try out. You should not miss these days of practice. They are vital to your "making the team." As former coaches we can tell you that coaches are going to be looking at several things. First and most obvious is your ability in that particular sport. Second, and not to be underrated, is all the "other" things, things like your attitude, your hustle, your positive character, and your "coachability." Many times these factors make the difference between someone making the team or not.

Finally an important fact for you to know before trying out is which sports make cuts and which sports do not. For example, some schools keep all the students who come out for cross country or freshman football, while others make cuts. Find this information out beforehand so it will help you make a decision about which sports to try out for.

Whatever happens when you try out for a sports team, whether or not you make the team, is secondary to the experience you gain from trying to make the team. Another experience in your life that helps you "build character," make new friends, and continues your path in a positive transition to high school.

Chapter Five

How to Form Positive School Relationships

We must, indeed, all hang together or, most assuredly, we shall all hang separately. —Benjamin Franklin

When twelfth graders get ready to graduate, the seniors who have had a great high school experience can easily name four or five faculty members who have made a difference to them throughout their high school years. The list of faculty members is never the same from senior to senior. In fact, usually there is a wide variety of staff members who have made a difference in the lives of the different students. There is solid research that has been done to prove that the significant, healthy connections you make with teachers, coaches, counselors, and other faculty members at high school will make your educational experience more positive and the more connected you will feel to the high school. Our personal experience tells us quite simply that you'll enjoy high school much more if you have formed these positive school relationships.

MAKING LIFE EASIER

It's not just fun to get along with teachers, coaches, and other staff members; it has real benefits as well. Part of handling the complexity of a high school is to be able to skillfully create advocates to help you. An advocate is someone who looks out for you, is in your corner, and will give you great advice when things aren't going so well. What most students don't even know is that these advocates are often looking out for their "favorites," even when the student doesn't know he or she needs it. Do you wonder why some students are nominated to serve on school committees or get special awards? Often, such recognition

Heather Rosen

Developing great relationships with teachers is well worth the time and effort.

results from a teacher or coach's mentioning a favored student to the principal and then, as a result, the student is selected for an award or distinction. We have seen countless successful students who have the right people in their corner so that when they needed help or assistance, just the right person was there to help them. Remember, teachers are regular people who respond to courtesy, respect, and genuine kindness. They remember those who give extra effort to forge positive relationships with them.

DON'T GET LOST IN THE SHUFFLE

Although high schools in America can be different sizes, usually your high school will have more students than your middle school. We have seen some ninth grade students enter high school and become completely overwhelmed simply by the sheer size of the school and the number of students attending. With more students and a bigger building to deal with, the especially smart ninth graders take some proactive steps to make sure they don't get "lost." Of course, when we say "lost," we don't mean physically getting lost (although that happens sometimes in high school). We mean getting lost in the transition to high school by not connecting with anything or anyone. Take steps not to get "lost" by making the connections with adults in the building. This will help you make the transition to the high school smoothly. Say "hello" to adults in the building. Use good manners. Experts have done research on this topic and the results are clear. Students who make a meaningful healthy connection with at least one faculty member tend to have a much more positive overall high school experience.

For some of you these types of connections with adults occur naturally. You have always been at ease with teachers and others at the school. For others, connecting with teachers may be something you hate doing. You'd rather just be friends with other teenagers, and you might be intimidated by the adults. Trust us; it is worth the effort to reach out to the adults in your school. You never know how it will help you in the future.

EASY TIPS FOR CREATING POSITIVE RELATIONSHIPS WITH SCHOOL STAFF

The following suggestions come from years of experience watching and witnessing teenagers just like you. Some handle this topic very well, while others handle it poorly. We have learned from all of them. What follows are a few simple, easy tips to help you in your journey toward building relationships with faculty members.

Always Treat Faculty and Staff at the School with Respect

One comment we hear from teenagers when talking about showing respect is, "I show someone respect when they show me respect." While we understand why you might say this or believe it, the reality is that the opposite attitude will build your credibility among school staff. Remember that the adults in the building are human beings also. If you treat a staff member with respect and dignity, word of your positive attitude will travel fast among teachers. Of course, the opposite is also true. If you are disrespectful to a teacher (even if you feel the teacher was being disrespectful toward you), the rest of the faculty will soon learn of it, and that is not a good thing!

Go Out of Your Way to Thank Faculty and Staff Who Do Simple Things for You

We hope that the words in the heading above seem obvious to you, but you would probably be shocked to know that many teens overlook saying a simple, "Thank you," when a faculty or staff member does or says something they should appreciate. You want to be especially aware of people who may not always get the recognition from others, such as secretaries or custodians. Believe it or not, these staff members can really look out for you in certain situations; therefore, you want to make sure they view you as a person who is appreciative of what they do each day.

Don't Be Afraid to Ask Adults for Help

Just about every adult in the school building works there because they enjoy working with kids and will offer help when needed. Some teenagers make the vital mistake of believing they can handle everything themselves and try to solve all their own problems. It is true that, to some extent, you should be becoming more independent in high school. But as adults, we ask people for help all the time! Sometimes the mature thing to do is to seek assistance when you are unsure or confused, or just need some advice.

By asking for help from school staff members (teachers, administrators, secretaries, counselors, etc.), you will accomplish so many positives. First, you show your maturity to the adult staff member. Second, you have one more interaction with that adult to help them remember you. Third, you will get help in whatever you needed in the first place.

Asking for help can range from needing academic help from your teacher to asking the security person to help open your locker or asking the secretary to explain the process for checking out for a doctor's appointment. For the purpose of establishing positive relationships at school, the reason you are asking for help isn't as important as the fact that you're actually asking for the help.

Get Involved

All of Chapter 4 is dedicated to how and why you should get involved with your school outside the normal classroom activities. It is important to know that by getting involved in activities, clubs, and sports you will create more advocates for yourself. If you have a problem with a teacher and you're not sure how to handle the situation, you can go to your coach or your band teacher to ask for guidance and help when dealing with the situation. Getting involved in other school activities will create countless positive and supportive connections, which is a huge benefit, one that will help you in many ways. So…get involved!

Have a Sense of Humor

Despite what you see in movies about high school teachers, most of them love their jobs and enjoy working with teenagers. Having a sense of humor is extremely important as you develop positive relationships with teachers, coaches, administrators, and other faculty members. There are times when a good sense of humor will help you develop those relationships and enhance the development of your relationships with teachers in the building.

Here are a couple of warnings about this hint. First, remember that you are the student and the teacher is the adult. Sometimes when a teacher shows a sense of humor, students mistake this behavior to mean they can be more informal with the teacher and perhaps even fail to show the teacher the proper respect. Be careful not to blur the line between you and the teacher. Don't ever allow yourself to forget that your teacher is not your peer or buddy. Even though you might get along with the teacher very well and notice that the teacher relates to teenagers extremely well, you have to remember that he or she is still the teacher. Don't let your sense of humor go too far, or even tease the teacher too much with jokes as you might with a friend or fellow student. Always remain aware of when it's time to stop with jokes and humor. In other words, during class time (or practice), there are times when you have to get to work. If you keep cracking jokes or laughing, it will quickly backfire. You will then establish a negative relationship with that teacher rather than the positive one you are working on.

FIVE IMPORTANT PEOPLE WITH WHOM TO FORM A POSTIVE RELATIONSHIP OTHER THAN THE TEACHERS

Your teachers will be the most important people, and they will have the greatest impact on your academic life for the next four years. Naturally teachers will be the most essential positive relationships you will form as you transition to high school. However, the following five people can also have a great impact on your life, and they can assist you in so many ways. Don't expect to establish these bonds the first week of school, but keep in mind the importance of eventually getting to know these people.

- **Your Guidance Counselor** – You will have a guidance counselor assigned to you when you enter high school. The assignments might be done by alphabet (first letter of your last name) or by grade level. In any case, you will have one. Your guidance counselor will be so important to you during high school from scheduling your classes to helping you if you are struggling (academically, socially, family issues, etc.). What you need to know is that this person has many, many students assigned to his or her caseload. While they want to help everyone, sometimes the number of students they are working with makes that impossible. That means you need to do something to set yourself apart from others so that your guidance counselor especially looks out for you. We suggest that sometime in October of your freshman year, if you haven't had any other meetings with your counselor, set up a 5-minute appointment to introduce yourself. Don't set this up in August or September as usually the counselors are super busy making sure their students' schedules are correct.

- **Coach or Club Sponsor** – Did we mention that you should get involved with your high school outside the regular classroom environment? You will learn things about life outside the classroom every day. Coaches and club sponsor will have a big influence on you.
- **School Secretaries** – Most likely there will be a few key secretaries that can really help you during your transition to high school and throughout your high school career. You will have a secretary assigned to you by alphabet (first letter of your last name) or by grade level. This person will help with many logistics (checking in and out of school, etc.). Many teenagers overlook these important staff members. Try going out of your way to say, "thank you," getting them a card during Administrative Professional Day, or just stopping by to see them on a Friday and say, "Have a good weekend!" These thoughtful actions will make you special in their eyes. This positive difference will come in handy when you need a favor or help down the road.
- **Athletic Director/Activities Director (AD)** – This person is another often overlooked person by the normal teenager. If you are involved in athletics, the Athletic Director does so many things behind the scenes to help you. This work is often underappreciated. You might not get to know the A.D. right away, but this person is another great advocate to have in your corner in case you need help or assistance with any issues related to athletics.
- **School Principal (or Administrator)** – As school principals we can tell you that your principal is really busy. Most likely he or she is under a lot of pressure to run a good school, meet testing objectives, and, in general, is responsible for everything that occurs in your school; however, keep in mind that most school principals used to be teachers. In general, the reason they got into education was because they wanted to help teenagers.

Therefore, interactions with students (like you) are usually the best part of their day.

Here's a true story to help you get to know your school principal. We have both had students use this technique successfully with us. This specific example is told from Alex's perspective (of course, the student name has been changed).

A few years ago, a new student walked up to me during the first week of school and said, "Are you the principal?" When I confirmed this, she said, "Nice to meet you. My name is Samantha Watkins." She then smiled and half-jokingly said, "I hope you will remember my name. Will you be able to do that?" I have to admit, being the principal of a large high school makes it difficult to know every student who attends, let alone remember all of their names! But when this young lady informally challenged me to remember her name, it really got my attention.

Not only did she do this on the first day, she followed up with this challenge. She came back to me the next day and playfully asked if I remembered her name. Luckily for me, I did! But don't be surprised if your principal doesn't remember your name on the first try. Reintroduce yourself. Go back in two days and ask again, always with a smile on your face. Pretty soon your principal will not only remember your name, but will have a good feeling about you too.

Remember – principals are human beings too! They want to have connections with students. Make sure you always say hello to your principal whenever you happen to run into each other. We bet that pretty soon you will be on great terms with this important school leader. We bet that your friends will wonder how you got to know the principal so fast! And by doing this you will have created a positive relationship with the person in charge of the school, and you never know when that relationship will come in handy!

- **Bonus Person – The School Nurse** – If you have severe medical allergies or other serious medical issues, it is vital for you to establish a positive relationship with the school nurse. Your school most likely will require you to have some sort of Health

Treatment Plan (not as complicated as it sounds) to assist you if you ever have a medical emergency at school. Obviously, the nurse is your key resource and advocate in these situations. Make sure you (and your parents) meet with the school nurse before school starts so that she is aware of your medical issues and can assist you appropriately when needed.

IT'S OKAY IF YOU DON'T GET ALONG WITH EVERYONE

In a perfect world you would get along beautifully with all your teachers and all the staff members at your school. This is not reality, and you should not panic if you don't click with all your teachers. Keep in mind that you still want to try to forge a positive relationship (especially with a teacher) because not doing so can make for a very long year in that class, resulting in a negative impact on you emotionally and academically. Do your best to follow our suggestions to make the relationship positive.

If, however, it's a lost cause and things are going badly for whatever reason, we suggest you get help from your counselor and your parents. It's better to ask for help earlier rather than later. Sometimes disagreements can be solved when brought to people's attention early. If you wait too late, things tend to get worse and solutions are much harder to develop at that point.

Chapter Six

How to Keep Your Teachers Happy

Over the next four years you are likely to work with somewhere between 24 and 32 different high school teachers. Your overall high school experience will be greatly enhanced by your skillful handling of these teachers and their different personalities. Keeping your teachers happy will lead to a positive classroom experience, better grades, and help your high school years to be successful.

If you are like many teens getting ready to enter high school, you have heard "stories" about how mean and difficult high school teachers can be with their students. Not to worry, these "stories" most likely are overblown. They tend to be like urban legends, and they grow more exaggerated over time. No doubt your eighth grade teachers have probably told you such things as, "You won't be able to get away with that next year in high school," or "High school teachers will not accept that from you; you'll get a zero."

We're here to help you deal with the anxiety of working with high school teachers. Following our suggestions (and remember these suggestions really come from the most savvy high school students we have watched over the years), will give you an edge in connecting with your teachers, understanding them, and having the relationship between yourself and the teacher pay off for you in the long run!

SOME BASIC UNDERSTANDINGS ABOUT HIGH SCHOOL TEACHERS

Remember that at some point all high school teachers chose their profession because they wanted to work with teenagers and felt they could make a difference. While it is true that at the high school level many teachers also really love the content they are teaching, they first and foremost became teachers because they want to work with young people like you! It is important to keep this in mind no matter what the teacher's reputation might be, how the teacher may appear on the outside, or how many years the teacher has been teaching.

Teachers you will work with will have personalities that range all across the spectrum, and they will each have different levels of expertise and experience. As a maturing young adult, you are more aware of all these factors now then you were when you were younger. For example, in first grade, you really enjoyed your teacher because she was your teacher and she cared about you and you loved being in her classroom no matter her age, or experience, or reputation. Be fair to each teacher you come into contact with. Don't allow any perceptions or preconceived thoughts influence your initial ideas about your teachers.

In general, what high school teaches want is simple. They want students who care about learning, do their work, be respectful, resist being disruptive, and have fun learning. Your high school teachers want to feel like they are making a difference for you and a positive influence on your life.

GROUND RULES FOR THE CLASSROOM

In high school (like elementary and middle school), teachers deserve to always be treated with respect. We are not telling you that you always have to agree with or like everything a teacher says or expects from you. We are telling you that you must show respect to your teachers no matter what. (Really, you should show respect to all adults in the school for that matter.) Students who are disrespectful to their teachers quickly gain a reputation among the faculty, which will hurt your chances of success and your positive experience in high school.

Every teacher wants to be treated with respect. If you disagree with a teacher or don't like how they are treating you, there are appropriate ways to handle this situation. The savviest students are able to stand up for what they believe in and make their points without becoming disrespectful. Never confront a teacher in front of the entire class. When you have serious issues to discuss with the teacher or you believe the teacher is treating you unfairly, handle this privately in a one-on-one environment. It is also useful to enlist the support of your guidance counselor or parent.

THE FIRST DAY

There is a common expression that says, "You never a get a second chance to make a first impression." The teacher's impression of you starts the moment you walk into the classroom on the first day of school. Of course, some teachers will have assigned seating, but others will allow you to choose where to sit. Do not sit in the back row. Relax, we're not saying you need to sit front and center either. Find a place you are comfortable with, but if you go to the back row, the teacher may make a judgment about you already. (It may not be a fair one, but they will still make it.) Think about it: Traditionally, who chooses to sit in the back row? Teachers will assume that the students who choose to sit in the back row aren't serious about school.

Insider's Tip: On the first day of school, if you have a choice, sit anywhere but in the last row. Students that choose to sit in the last row send a negative signal to the teacher.

On the first day of school your teacher is excited. As corny as it sounds, many teachers can't sleep the night before the first day of school because they are ready to meet their new students and start the new year off on the right foot. If you come in with a frown on your face, without saying a word and sit in the back row, you have sent a clear message to the teacher. The message that the teacher interprets is that this is a student who doesn't want to be here, doesn't respect me or my class. We understand that these judgments are not fair to make. As high school insiders we're telling you that these are the thoughts that are going on in the teacher's head. Students can overcome these initial negative thoughts, but why present yourself in a negative light?

As a savvy new student to high school, you want to walk into each class on the first day in a positive way, saying "hello" to the teacher and anticipating that you will have to play the game of the first day of school. In other words, "playing the game" of school means knowing that on the first day, teachers generally go over rules, expectations, and policies. It's not the most exciting stuff in the world! If you anticipate this beforehand, and accept it, than don't be negative about it with the teacher. (It's okay to be negative inside, just don't let it show on the outside.)

Remember your goal on the first day is to stay positive; not doing anything that would cast a negative light on you from the teacher (like sitting in the back row or disrupting the class). Be polite and, no matter what you're feeling on the inside, have a smile on your face and be excited to be starting high school.

HOW TO HANDLE YOURSELF IN THE CLASSROOM

Remember what we have said about high school teachers: Each one is different. A skilled student uses these differences to his or her advantage. In other words, how you handle yourself in the classroom should be based on the personality of the teacher. However, there are some principles that are universal. These principles can assist you with a positive healthy relationship with the teacher and enhance your chances of success not only in this particular class, but also in high school.

Make the Teacher Believe You Are Interested in the Subject

Remember high school teachers majored in the subject area in college. That means they have a real interest and passion in the subject they teach. Nothing makes them happier than students who might show the same interest. We're not saying you have to become a Shakespearean scholar or a World War II history expert, but what we are saying is that during class time you want that teacher to know that your total focus is on that particular subject.

Participate Actively and Positively in Class

High school teachers will put time and energy into designing lessons for you. Teachers love students who appreciate their efforts. Showing your appreciation is simple. All you have to do is be an active participant in class. No matter the activity, make sure that you are not the student who gets mad or stands out as being negative. You don't have to be the most active student if you are not comfortable; just don't be the one who refuses to participate at all.

Go to the Teacher for Help

We suggest at some point all students should go to the teacher for extra help. In high school this doesn't mean you aren't smart. In fact, the smartest students in the toughest classes are usually the ones staying after school to get extra help from their teacher. More importantly, by going to the teacher for extra help, you send a clear message to the teacher. "I care about your class, and I care about my performance in your class." The discussion should not always be about your grade, but rather about your learning the material and performing better in the class.

Laugh at the Teacher's Jokes

This idea is sort of a silly one, but not to be underrated. Really, this suggestion means more than just laugh at the teacher's jokes. It shows your appreciation for your teacher's hard work each day. When they try to have fun or make learning interesting, go along with it. However, know when it is time to have fun and when it is time to get down to business. We have seen many students blur this line, and it

Insider's Tip: If you partially understand something, but not completely, go to the teacher after school for help. After the teacher assists you in understanding the material, explain it back to the teacher in your own words. Most importantly, make sure the teacher knows how thankful you are that they took the time to work with you. Say something like, "Thank you Mrs. Smith, I always struggled with this concept, but now I finally get it."

always leads to problems. Have fun when the teacher is joking, but don't be disrespectful. Don't go too far and become a distraction to the teacher or your classmates.

Show Appreciation for the Teacher

Do you remember in elementary school when you saw your teacher out at the grocery store and you were amazed? What was your first grade teacher doing shopping? She's supposed to always be in school. Teachers are people too. They have emotions; they have families; and they have problems just like everyone else. If you always remember that your teachers are persons who are trying their hardest to do the right thing for you and your classmates, then it will help you to always show your appreciation.

If you want to stand out in a positive way with your teacher try this tactic. After class one day that might have included a lesson that was particularly fun, go up to the teacher on your way out of the classroom. Quietly, without your classmates hearing, tell the teacher "thank you." Say something like this, "Mrs. Smith, I really enjoyed class today. Thanks for taking the time to develop that lesson." Okay, we know that sounds corny to you, but we cannot emphasize the positive points you will score with your teacher. None of your classmates need to know what you said to the teacher. You will make your teacher feel great and make you stand out in a positive way. You will be one of the few students who ever took the time to say, "Thank you."

THE PAYOFF

If you take the time to handle your teachers with skill and keep them happy, then they start to become your allies, people in the school who look out for you. In high school you never know when you will need adults in your corner. We are sure of one thing after working with teenagers: There are usually some problems along the way. Some are more serious than others. Having adults who care about you and able to assist you will be beneficial for you when you come across difficult times.

The other payoff is directly in that teacher's classroom. The reality is that some grades in high school are subjective. The more work you have done to positively contribute to class, stay on the teacher's good side, and make the classroom experience positive makes it more likely that the teacher will look out for you with your grades. This doesn't mean that a "D" will magically turn into an "A." It means that when you are a point away from the "A" the teacher will be more likely to give you a break because of your positive relationship and positive contributions to class.

Chapter Seven

How to Keep Your Parents Happy

If you are like most other teenagers in the country, you have recently entered the time in your life when power struggles between yourself and your parents become more and more frequent. You want more independence; you want to be treated like an adult; you want to hang out with your friends more often; and quite honestly, your parents embarrass you sometimes. This struggle is typical and has been going on since the beginning of time. In fact, whether or not you believe it, your parents went through the same struggle with their parents.

After working in high schools for so many years, we have seen how really skilled teens managed this struggle masterfully so that they keep their parents happy (most of the time at least) and become able to enjoy many of the freedoms they want as young adults.

This struggle really can be summed up briefly: You feel like you should be able to do what you want to do and be able to handle things on your own. Your parents feel like you're still a child and need their guidance and support.

WHY DO PARENTS ACT LIKE THIS?

It's important to understand that your parents, no matter how strict they seem to be, are making their decisions based on one simple fact. They love you. You are their child, and they are trying to help you make the best decisions for your future. They are scared and anxious as you enter high school since they know how important this time is for you. They don't want to see you "mess it up." So, no matter what, no matter how much they frustrate you or make decisions you believe are unfair, remember they are doing it because they believe it's the

Gregory Johnston

Even when you don't feel like listening -- listen! Your parents are smarter than you think.

right thing for you. They are doing it because they love you.

As they make these decisions (out of love), keep in mind that there is no instruction book on how to raise children. There is no magical formula for success. If there ever was such a formula, every parent would act the same way and make the same decisions to ensure the success of his or her teenager. The reality is that each family is different, and each teenager (that's you) is different. So, parents try to make the best decisions for you and your family based on what they think is right.

SOME PARENTAL GROUND RULES

You're probably not going to love what we write next, but we feel it is important to remind you of a few things before discussing strategies to help you get more of what you want from your parents and have them treat you more like an adult. That's really our goal here: to help you understand your parents and give you ideas to make them happy. In turn, you can get the freedoms you feel you deserve to prove that you are able to handle the responsibility of becoming an adult.

In most cases, as you go through high school, you will be living in your parents' house, eating food they have purchased for you, and wearing clothes they will buy for you. So, what does that mean? It means that, like it or not, your parents are ultimately in charge. They get to make the rules, and you will be expected to follow them. Teenagers hate to hear this, but it is true. Yes, it might be your bedroom, but really, it's their house, which makes it their bedroom they are letting you use. Our point is that you will need to continue to follow their rules unless you plan to move out, pay your own rent, pay for food, clothing, transportation, cable bill, technology use, etc. (We strongly advise against these actions.) Besides, in many states, you will need to do some serious legal work to become legally emancipated from your parents' guardianship, so it is most likely a moot point anyway.

Now that you have accepted that your parents are in charge of the house, let's focus on how to get the most privileges and the most freedoms that you want.

ACADEMIC EXPECTATIONS

Your parents are normal if they have academic expectations for you. These expectations should be established based on your goals and potential. Let's remember the number one reason you're going to high school is to get a good education and be ready for the next stage of life (college, military, work, etc.). Not every student is expected to get straight "A's" and be in the most advanced classes. This type of expectation is different for everyone. All that parents want you to do is work up to your potential.

Of course, the most important part of this step is to make sure you understand what your parents' expectations are and what your personal expectations are for your grades. As we discussed in Chapter 2, "The Importance of a Good Plan," it's important for you and your parents to have had this discussion before the school year starts to ensure that you know exactly what you need to do.

Accomplishing this means that you must stay motivated, work hard, and make sure to clearly communicate with your parents. Often times, we have dealt with students who have not worked up to their potential, and in turn, their parents are unhappy, causing the relationship at home to become more restrictive and tense. One of the first things we ask these students is, "Are you working as hard as you can?"

The Benefit of Working Up to Your Potential

We have worked with many students who have failed to realize the side benefits of working up to their potential and getting good grades (again, not necessarily straight "A's," but good grades as defined by your family). When we say side benefits, we're referring to all the other benefits beside the academic ones. The academic benefits should be obvious. Benefits like getting good grades in ninth grade prepare you for your tenth grade classes. Benefits like being savvy enough to know that the grades you get your freshman year mean just as much to your grade point average as your junior and senior years. Benefits like getting good grades will make your transcript look better for colleges and universities when you begin to apply to get into such schools. In short, academically getting good grades opens doors for you and gives you more options when you make decisions about your life as you get older.

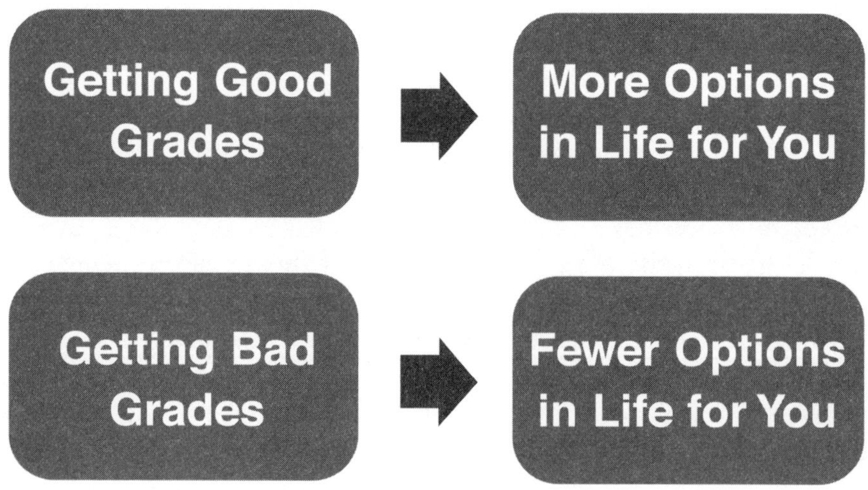

The Side Benefit of Working Up to Your Potential

There is a whole side benefit to working up to your potential and getting good grades that really has nothing to do with your future. Rather, it has to do with getting what you want right now. The concept is simple, yet many teenagers do not understand it and miss the opportunity to make their lives easier at home. Let's illustrate this concept to you by asking a few questions.

Question #1 - If you bring home a good report card, will that make your parents happy or angry with you?

Question #2 – When your parents are happy with you, do they tend to be more lenient or stricter with you?

Question #3 – When your parents are more lenient with you, do you get to do more things you want to do?

If you were honest when answering the above questions, it seems obvious that getting good grades will lead your parents to making decisions that will benefit you. (Remember that good grades are defined by your potential and do not necessarily have to be perfect.) We have seen it time and time again, when parents see their teenager trying his or her hardest in school and achieving good grades, then those teens tend to get more privileges, such as later curfews and more freedom to hang out with friends. Sometimes these positive grades let your parents see that you can handle the responsibility of more adult-like things (like the latest cell phone, computer, or even getting a license to drive when you are eligible).

You have to understand how parents think in these situations so you can increase your chances to get to do more of the things you want to do as a teenager. Trust us, parents are not as complicated as you might think in these situations. If you get good grades, your parents will tend to give you more independence because grades are one way to prove to them that you can handle adult responsibilities. Remember, it's not the only way to prove your maturity, and you certainly can ruin the positive feelings generated by good grades by making other bad decisions, but getting good grades can be a huge benefit for you and your life around the house.

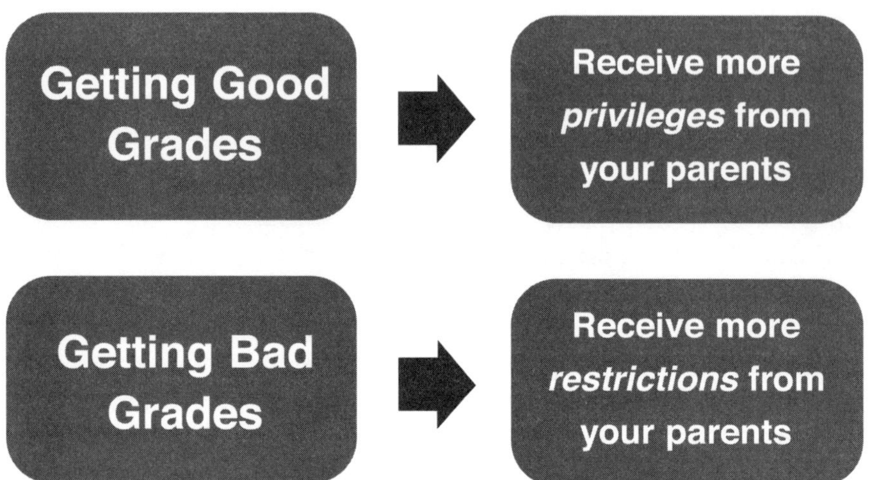

If you get bad grades or a bad report card, your parents will take that as a sign you cannot handle some of the responsibilities of becoming an adult. This will result in their tending to be more restrictive.

How Do I Repair Things if I Don't Work Up to My Potential?

Don't despair if you struggle with your grades as you begin high school. Transitioning to high school is one of the most difficult things you will do in your life. It is difficult and stressful for everyone, including your parents. Some teens handle it better than others. If you don't, it is normal and most importantly, it is repairable.

First, academically speaking, if your grades are not where you want them to be, read Chapter 8, "Monitoring Your Progress." This chapter will give you some practical tips on how to get assistance and what resources to use to get your grades back on track.

Second, you need to understand a few things about your parents to be able to repair this damage, or better yet, minimize your parents' frustration with you if your grades are not good enough. Most parents do not like surprises. So, one strategy you should use is that when your grades begin to falter, make sure your parents are aware of this issue. Many schools today have on-line student information systems that will allow your parents access to your grades and attendance on a daily basis. If this is the case in your high school, then your parents may be well informed if you start to get some low grades. However, nothing will speak more to your potential maturity than when you ask your parents if you could have a talk with them and then tell them about your academic struggles before they get a report card and before they bring the issue up with you.

This action is not an easy one for most teenagers. We understand, but we are going to give you a great strategy to help a bad situation. To help the situation we are going to give you some specific ideas about what to say during this conversation.

When you approach your parents about this conversation, it is best to have already thought through what you want to say, and you should anticipate what they are going to say. Diagnose the problem.

"Mom and Dad, I need to talk to you about my ______ class. I'm having a tough time in the class, and I've gotten a few low grades on my writing assignments which have made my grade lower than I want it to be."

Of course, you need to adapt the above statement to fit your situation. The reason your grades might be low could be for many different reasons, such as not turning in homework or not paying attention in class. You might also feel that the tests are too hard, you just don't get the material, or you might be having an overall difficult time in all of your classes. Whatever the reason, be honest with your parents. Remember, it is normal for them to be concerned, but they will be extremely impressed about the way in which you approached this situation. Also, understand that they aren't going to just say, "Ok, thanks for telling us. We'll talk to you later."

So, next have a potential solution for the problem.

"I spoke to my English teacher, Mrs. Madison, and she said I could come after school one day a week starting next week to work on my writing skills. I'm going to take the school's activity bus which will get me home from school later. Is this OK with you guys?"

Again, you will have to adapt the above statement to fit your individual situation, but having a potential solution already thought through will earn huge points for you. Your solution may involve being more organized (like using your planner we suggested in Chapter 3 – "Get Yourself Organized"), or your solution may involve a commitment to pay attention more during class and improve your note-taking. Your solution may also involve telling your parents that you have a plan for completing homework every night. Whatever the plan, the key is for you to have a plan that you can share with your parents.

Keep in mind that your parents may still have their own suggestions and ideas to help you get out of the hole you are in. You may like some of their ideas; and you may hate others. Be careful with your reaction to their ideas - an outwardly negative reaction could damage all the good will you have created with your earlier statements. Sit politely and listen to their ideas and advice. Don't say, "You don't know what you are talking about" or "That is stupid!" Remember, these discussions are often going to be their first try at figuring out how they can help you recover. If you don't like an idea, calmly explain to them why you think this won't work. Reassure them that you appreciate their help and concern. If you react negatively to their suggestions, you might actually be "making a mountain out of molehill," or in other words, a big deal out of a small issue. Never forget that your parents are going to give you lots of advice (that's one of their jobs!). Sometimes you will want to make them happy by sitting patiently and listening politely to their input. This will benefit you so that you can discuss any issue and, together, know that you can come up with a solution that suits everyone.

An important note in this discussion is to make sure you understand that if all of your grades are low and you are feeling overwhelmed or totally stressed out, you need to speak openly and honestly with your parents and a guidance counselor at your school. The earlier a problem like this is dealt with, the quicker you can get help from school staff and your family. There is plenty of help out there for students. You just need to make sure you ask for it earlier rather than later in the year.

The last thing to keep in mind about repairing any damage when your grades are not indicative of your potential is that, after you have met with your parents, diagnosed the problem, and mapped out the problem, you need to actually solve the problem. You don't want to come back to your parents in a few weeks and have your grades still remaining low, especially if you didn't follow through with the plan you developed to help the situation.

BEHAVIORAL EXPECTATIONS

As we said earlier about academic expectations, expect your parents (if they are normal) to have behavioral expectations for you as well as you enter high school. The struggle between parent and teenager over how much freedom is allowed has been going on for a long time. (Your parents went through it with their parents too!) So, to keep in line with our basic idea, keeping your parents happy and hoping that things will be better at home, we are going to give you some strategies to navigate this difficult period of time that occurs in every household. These strategies come from teenagers just like you whom we have watched with admiration as they skillfully kept their parents happy and, in turn, were allowed more freedoms. We have tried to group these strategies within so-called trouble areas.

Before we get into these areas, keep in mind that every house, every parent, and every teenager is different. Your parents will have different rules than the parents of your friends. This is normal. Your parents are trying to make the best rules for you and your family.

Curfews

Expect that your parents will have a curfew for you on school nights and weekend nights. As a rising ninth grader you will not (and should not) receive the same curfew as juniors or seniors. Curfews are one of those things that, no matter what time a parent sets, the teenager always wants it to be later. You will have some friends who have later curfews, earlier curfews, and some who will have no curfews. Remember that your parents are deciding on a curfew based on what they believe is the right time for you and your family.

After years of working with high school students, we can tell you that we've have heard countless stories about bad decisions people make late at night (or better put, in the early hours of the next morning). We have heard of students getting in big-time trouble, getting arrested, and in general acting foolish in these late hours. There is a saying that goes like this, "Nothing good happens after midnight. After midnight is when good people make bad decisions."

"How Do I Get a Later Curfew?"

Keep our thinking in mind as we discuss the question of how you can try to get a later curfew from your parents. The week after your parents set the original curfew is probably not the time to try to negotiate a later one. Realistically, your chances of getting a later curfew are down the road. We have seen teens succeed by taking these two steps. First, they honor the original curfew by always being home by the established time. Your parents are evaluating your maturity all the time. Ask yourself this question: If you tell your parents you are going to the pool and they tell you that you need to be home by 6:00 pm and you don't show up at home until 8:00 pm with no phone call, are your parents going to trust you to understand the concept of time limits? When you try later to negotiate a new curfew, they will remember how you have handled smaller freedoms before.

The second step in your attempt to get a later curfew is that after a period of time (think end of freshman year), you go to your parents and ask if you could have a meeting with them about your curfew. By taking the "formal" step of setting a meeting you take the edge off of the discussion, show your parents that you are mature, and minimize the chances that the discussion will turn ugly.

When you sit down for the meeting, tell your parents that you understand they may have to think about this and that you will understand if they don't make a decision right now. (Your parents will really like this.) Next, remind your parents with specific examples, if you can, of how you have honored their current curfew expectation. Use good grades and the fact that you haven't gotten into any trouble as part of your evidence that you can handle the responsibility of a later curfew. Finally, don't ask them to extend your curfew ridiculously. (*"Can I come home 3 hours later?")* Instead, ask them to extend your curfew by something reasonable. We suggest starting small, maybe by extending the curfew by 30 minutes.

If this strategy doesn't work, then we suggest that you see if your parents will consider a "trial" basis of a later curfew so you can prove that you are responsible. Possibly you could ask for a "big event" one-time extension. If all of these strategies fail, ask your parents what you can do to prove you can handle the privilege of a later curfew. Keep in mind that sometimes parents just won't budge on this issue. As much as you don't want to hear this, you have to realize they are in charge and have the prerogative. They set the rules in your house.

Friends

Another classic area for controversy between you and your parents will be your friends. The battle between a teen's loyalty to friends and loyalty to family is a normal situation in most households. Keep in mind that your family should always be your number one priority. Your family will always be with you through good times and bad times. Unfortunately, we can't always say the same thing about friends. We have worked with many teenagers who had different struggles about all different things, and we have sadly watched as their closest friends deserted them. Don't get us wrong; you will make some great friends in high school. (Maybe you've already started to establish these friendships.) But our point is that your family should always be top priority to you.

It is normal for your parents to want to meet your friends and know who you are hanging out with. A great way to keep your parents happy about your friends is to talk about them at home (no matter how many times your mom or dad may ask you, "Who is

Andrew again?"). By having open conversations about your friends, your parents will notice that you are open about them and not trying to hide anyone from them. The second part of this strategy is to introduce them to your parents. They can come by your house to meet your parents, or you can introduce them at some school event.

The Big Ones

We know that as a teenager you are already aware of the big things that can get you in serious trouble both at home and at school. Most school divisions have very serious consequences assigned to infractions such as drugs, alcohol, weapons, violence, threats of violence, and other serious things. Unfortunately, in our roles as school administrators, we have seen many "good kids" make bad choices and, in turn, change their lives for the worse. We have seen teenagers just like you get involved in bad stuff trying to impress someone. We have seen students, who get good grades and don't have any discipline issues, make a quick impulsive decision because their "friend" was doing something. We have seen teenagers try something because they think they won't get caught (but they do!).

Getting involved in the serious infractions really can have a life-altering impact on you. We know that just about every teenager in America will be exposed to friends or people they know who will make bad decisions about these serious things and, in turn, you will be faced with the temptation or the pressure to participate. Here's what we'll tell you after working with high-school-aged teenagers for many years. The savvy students have a plan to gracefully separate themselves from their friends when the group starts participating in activities they know will get them in trouble.

Think about this issue another way. Your family (even though they might get on your nerves) should be the most important people to you in the whole world. Friends come and go, girlfriends and boyfriends will come and go, but through it all, your family is always there. Your education should also be pretty important. After all (as we have explained in previous chapters), your education will open up all sorts of options and increase your earning power as you get older and take charge of your life as an adult. When you get involved with the serious things that can get you in big-time trouble at home and at school, you simply pull yourself away from your family and your schooling. It's that simple. In fact, getting involved with some of these negative things at school might cost you your ability to be in control of your own future.

AROUND THE HOUSE

Since this is a chapter about keeping your parents happy we thought we should just make a quick mention about life around your house and some quick reminders that will make your life easier as you transition to high school. It is normal for your parents to have some basic expectations for you. For example, making your bed and cleaning your room are some of these expectations. For many teenagers we understand that this is quite a challenge. We also understand it is source of much parental frustration. If you attend to these chores without making it a big deal, then things will be better for you.

If you are expected to complete certain chores around the house, then it would be a good idea to continue doing these things without argument. Again, completing these chores without being asked shows your parents that you are a mature member of the household. Following this advice can only bring good things for you!

We are sure there are other simple basic things you will be expected to do around the house. Don't make a big deal out of minor issues. It's easier sometimes just to do these things for the good of the family and to keep your parents happy. Remember that the happier they are with you, the better chance you will have to get more privileges because of your proven responsibility.

CONVERSATION AND COMMUNICATION

Finally, and maybe the most important issue when trying to keep your parents happy, is communicating with them. We understand that for teenagers the ability to communicate, with your friends almost constantly is important. We also understand that family conversations do not always appeal to you. The lack of communication or your isolation from your parents will lead to problems. To keep your parents happy, the following sections describe three times during the day you can communicate with your parents and make them happy.

"What Did You Do in School Today?"

When you came home from your first day of Kindergarten, your parents asked, "What did you do in school today?" (Trust us. You may not remember that day, but your parents have clear memories of it.) Guess what? You were more than happy to tell them every detail of every second of that day. As the years went by, your answers may have become vaguer when asked this question. Now your response might be like many others when asked this question: "Nothing."

As a savvy teenager who knows that keeping parents happy is a key ingredient to happiness in your life, you should anticipate this question. Every day when you go to high school, make it your personal mission to make a mental note of two or three things you actually learned. These items don't have to be anything huge or groundbreaking, just some specific items. So, maybe the conversation goes like this:

"What did you do in school today?"

"Well, in math we reviewed fractions, which was easy, since we learned that stuff in middle school; in history we started a unit on the Roman Empire; and in P.E. we ran a timed mile."

Your parents will be so impressed with your statement that they will be happy to know that, in fact, you did do something in school on that day. Your parents can be easy to figure out. They want to hear anything beside "nothing." When you give that answer, nothing good can come of it. They may conclude that you're not learning, you're sleeping through the school day, or your teachers are doing nothing during the school day. This only frustrates and troubles your parents. Trust us. By using this one simple technique, you improve your home life and your relationship with your parents.

Dinner Table

We know that not every family is able to eat the traditional family dinner together every evening anymore. Life has become just too hectic. When we say, "dinner table," we are referring to those moments in life when you are with your parents for 20 to 30 minutes and expected to communicate with them. With your family, this might be at dinner time or at other moments. Use this time skillfully by telling your parents funny stories from school about friends, interesting things a teacher may have done in the class room, or about practices or meetings you're attending. Turn off the TV and put away your music. Turn off your cell phone! Don't make these conversations more difficult then they need to be. Remember that something is better than nothing. Plus, expect that your parents will ask you questions. Don't get frustrated by this, or you'll ruin all the good will you have gained by having the conversation in the first place. One more thing, you might want to remember that your parents may or may not share your sense of humor about all things. Consider the stories you choose to tell carefully to ensure that they are suitable for family dinner table conversation.

Car Rides

Not every minute of every car ride with your parent needs to be filled with conversation. Sometimes people zone out or just have quiet time in the car, but keep in mind, car rides are great opportunities to have uninterrupted dialogue with your parents about issues or happenings in your life. Sometimes, if it's just you and your parent, car rides are a good opportunity to discuss issues that might be bothering you.

"Mom, you know our neighbor Hannah? It's weird because I feel like I've been friends with her for years, but now at high school, she just ignores me. I don't get it."

Of course, the discussions in the car don't always have to be about serious things. They can also just be time to laugh about something funny in school or, in general, keeping your parents in the loop as far as what is happening to you at school. If you spend the entire car ride listening to music or texting your friends, you've missed a great opportunity to make your parents happy (and, in turn, make your life better!).

Chapter Eight

Monitoring Your Progress

As you are now aware, you are entering a very important stage of your education and life. You are going to want to be keenly aware of how well (or not so well) you are doing in the various aspects of your life. There is no shame in struggling academically, in sports or activities, or even socially during your freshman year. The real shame comes only if you are struggling and completely unaware that you are struggling. In this chapter, we will talk about how you can stay on top of your progress in all areas of your life. We'll start with the most common area of struggle for high school freshmen: academics.

MONITORING YOUR ACADEMIC PROGRESS

Time and again we've dealt with ninth graders and their parents after the first report card comes out. Four out of five times the parents' story goes something like this:

> Every day since school has started we've asked our ninth grader how school is going. Every day, we heard the same thing – "Great. Don't worry about it." Now we are nine weeks into the school year and we find out that he is failing four of his classes and barely passing the other three. We don't know how we got this far along without ever hearing anything from any of his teachers! Don't get us wrong, we are really upset with our son and place the responsibility for getting good grades on him, but this really surprised and upset us. How could this happen?

When we hear stories like this, we always wonder the same thing. We would love it if every time a student was struggling, the teachers immediately picked up the phone and called home, but we know this isn't always going to happen. Teachers in most high schools have 150 or more students. There is always a chance that a few will slip below the radar and really perform poorly without attracting any attention until it is too late. The reality is that the grade is the responsibility of the student, and the student should always be aware of where he or she stands in each of their classes. There are several ways that students can do this.

- Keep a running log of every assignment for each class in a notebook. Record the due dates for each assignment, the title for the assignment, when you turned the assignment in, when the assignment was returned to you, and the grade you received on each assignment in the log. If possible, find out how much each assignment is weighted in the calculation of the final grade for the grading period. If you follow this procedure, you should always know roughly where you stand in every class and will be on top of it if you start to struggle.
- Find out how to log in to the online student data system your school uses. It is likely that your parents have already got this access. You will be able to log on with your parents to review your academic data regularly allowing you to see your electronic grade book for each of your teachers as well as your attendance and other information. By logging on with your parents, you will be on the "same page" with respect to how things are going in school. There will be no surprises at report card time. Remember, however, that sometimes it takes days or even a week or two for teachers to update and make all of the grades current. Don't rely on the electronic information exclusively. Your daily participation in class will often give you a better picture of where you stand.
- Ask for weekly progress reports from teachers to keep you updated and on top of your status. Most schools offer a form

for teachers to fill out at the end of each week that includes your current grade. It also asks your teacher to rate your weekly conduct and effort in the class. This information can be useful to show your parents how you are doing, especially if you have been struggling and want to show that you are making progress toward improving your grades.

If at any time you determine that your grades are dipping in any of your classes, our best advice to you is to act swiftly. Don't wait to see if your grade is going to recover naturally. Sometimes waiting creates a situation where you are down too deep to make a recovery by the end of the grading period. If you are worried about your grade in a class, follow these steps:

1. Tell your parents that you are worried about how you are doing in one of your classes. (See Chapter 7.)
2. Schedule an appointment with your teacher to discuss your status in class. Ask the teacher what additional help he or she could offer to help you get back on track. Often great academic resources are available to you on the internet. (See Appendix A.) Also, ask if there is another student or resource you might use to help you gain mastery in areas where you are struggling.
3. Make a plan for how you will get back on track in the class. Discuss this plan with your parents and ask for their support/advice.
4. Establish a checkpoint for yourself a week or two away from the time you expect to have put yourself back in good standing in the class. If you are not on track to meet your deadline, go back to step one and begin again.

The bottom line is that you, the student, are the one who should always be on top of your academic standing in school. By keeping on top of it right from the start, being open and honest with your parents, and using the resources available to you at your school, you are most likely going to experience success right from the start. Ignorance of your academic status is never a good thing.

MONITORING YOUR NONACADEMIC SCHOOL LIFE

The most important thing to do in the nonacademic school life area is to keep a good line of communication open with everyone involved to ensure that you remain in good standing in any team, club, or organization in which you are involved. Periodically chat with your coach, sponsor, or activity director to make sure you are fulfilling all requirements of the organization. Attend all practices, meetings, and appointments expected of you, and if you can't, be sure to let the coach or sponsor know beforehand (if possible) or very soon afterwards why you weren't able to attend. Keep good contact with any student leaders/captains involved in your organization so that you know what is expected of you at all times. Often, this person will be the one to let you know most clearly if you are not keeping up with your commitments.

If you find that you are falling in to an academic, social, or emotional slump, Get help!

MONITORING YOUR SOCIAL/EMOTIONAL LIFE

The social/emotional life is an area where many high school freshmen struggle. They think they are the only ones having issues. It is not true! It is the rare fourteen- or fifteen-year-old who gets through this time without needing some support during the ninth grade year. It is really important and a good sign of maturity for ninth graders to do a periodic assessment of their social/emotional health. If you are often depressed, overly stressed out, or regularly making risky and unhealthy decisions, you should seek out help to find out what you can do to make sure you get your life back on track. The goal is for you to continue being the happy and successful person you deserve to be.

A good place to start is with your parents, the people who love and care about you most in the world. You should let them know what is going on and ask them for help dealing with any issues you can pinpoint. At first, this may be difficult, but these are the people who will stick with you through thick and thin, so count on them.

We know, however, that sometimes it is hard to talk to your parents about personal issues that many ninth graders face. Luckily for you, most schools have a number of resources available to students to help them manage and deal with non-academic issues.

A good person to start with is your guidance counselor. People who enter the field of counseling do so because they want to help people in trouble. Unfortunately, most counselors spend a great deal of time working with transcripts, college applications, and other paperwork. They are often searching for how they can make a real and tangible difference in the lives of students. They want to help you.

Another person most schools have on staff is a school psychologist. This person is not there for "crazy" people. They are there to help students deal with problems that may run a little deeper than typical issues. Often this person will become available to you after you have met with your guidance counselor, who may refer you to meet with this expert in personal development.

Many schools will have a drug and alcohol counselor to help students deal with issues relating to substance abuse. This person is a great resource for teens who find they have fallen into a dangerous and risky behavior pattern. Going to this person voluntarily is a great way to get help while avoiding having to deal with the ugly side of drug and alcohol use at school, which often results in serious disciplinary consequences.

Finally, there are often many unofficial resources you can go to for help. Any adult in the building (teachers, coaches, sponsors, etc.) will listen to you and give you advice on how to come up with solutions to solve any issues that arise. You need to hear a word of caution, however. School personnel are duty-bound to report issues if they feel you are making dangerous or risky decisions. Sometimes students think that there is confidentiality between students and adults in the building. There is not. In fact, school personnel are legally required to inform parents when they have information that a child is doing something that may endanger him or her. We are not saying this to scare you away from using adults at school as resources.

CONCLUSION

The bottom line is that you should know that whatever hurdles or obstacles you face as a high school student; you never have to face them alone. You have ample resources available to you. All that you need to do is to be aware enough to know if you are heading into troubled water, and then ask for help when you need it.

Chapter Nine

A Brief Look Forward

By the end of your first year in high school you'll be thinking, "Now that I finally have the ninth grade year figured out, I am moving on to tenth grade!" Don't worry too much about this. For the vast majority of high school students, the second year of high school, commonly called the "sophomore year," feels very, very similar to the ninth grade year. In this chapter we'll preview what you might expect during your tenth grade year in your academic, social, and family life. Finally, at the end of the chapter, we'll give you a brief warning and words of advice about the dreaded "sophomore slump."

ACADEMICS IN TENTH GRADE

Most ninth graders remark upon a significant change in the academic and intellectual demands that teachers expected of them between their final year in middle school and their first year in high school. You might also have felt that school work in ninth grade was more challenging and more time-consuming when compared with the work you were asked to do during your eighth grade year. The good news is that if you, through your organization, planning, and hard work, were able to successfully meet the expectations your ninth grade teachers put before you, you will find that tenth grade is a snap. We are not saying things get easier. It's just that you are now used to the workload and, usually, the degree of academic rigor in tenth grade is comparable to that of the ninth grade. Our advice to you is to maintain the good habits that you put in place during your ninth grade year and really use the tenth grade year to set yourself up for great success in the important eleventh grade, or junior year of high school.

SOCIAL LIFE IN THE TENTH GRADE

Just as you are likely to feel that you have it pretty well figured out when it comes to academics as you enter your tenth grade year, you will feel that you are on solid ground socially as well as you enter your second year in high school. Sophomores generally "know the score" and understand how the school works. You are likely to have established a good social network during your ninth grade year. This network will most likely remain in place during the second year of high school. You know how the social functions, such as dances and big games, generally go. You know where your classmates are likely to be sitting at lunch, and you know where to hang out before and after school. Most tenth graders generally feel at ease socially during this year because they are in the unique position of not being the "lowest on the totem pole" while having very little leadership expected of them during this year. Embrace your silly and immature side during this year. It is likely to be the last year of your life when you can act like a kid a lot of the time. Once you become a junior, both academically and socially, the stakes of the game will rise again, and you will be expected to behave more and more like an adult. Enjoy your sophomore year. It will be over before you know it!

FAMILY LIFE

Much like your academic and social life, family life during your sophomore year is likely to fall into the same comfortable patterns that existed during your freshman year. You are likely to have similar responsibilities and expectations as were in place during your ninth grade year. One event does often take place during the sophomore year that tends to change things somewhat: earning one's driver's license. This is often a signal to both the student and the parent that roles and responsibilities in the family are shifting. Once you accept your driver's license, you are also accepting that you will be expected to show more responsibility for both yourself and everyone else who travels with you in your car. You may also be expected to run errands and pick up your little brother or sister from practice. This is a great chance for you to impress your parents with your more mature attitude toward this very serious and important responsibility. Don't blow it by getting a speeding ticket or driving recklessly or dangerously in your first year of earning your driver's license!

THE DREADED "SOPHOMORE SLUMP"

It would be impossible for us to end this chapter without advising you to beware of the dreaded sophomore slump. First, let's talk about the origin of the term "sophomore." This word comes from the Greek roots, *sophos* and *moros. Sophos,* in Greek, is translated to "wisdom" or "wise." *Moros* is translated to "foolish." A loose interpretation of sophomore is "wise fool." From what we have seen in our careers, this is a great term for many tenth graders. Since they have spent a whole year in high school, they think they know everything there is to know about how high school works and don't really want any advice from anyone!

If we had a quarter for every time we've heard a tenth grader say, "You don't know what you're talking about" to their mother or father, we'd be rich men! Trust us. As tenth graders, you are still learning how to succeed in high school and need all the help you can get. Don't allow yourself to fall into a "sophomore slump" by thinking you are going to do it all on your own now that you are an experienced high school student. Continue to seek and accept advice and help from your parents and school advocates. In the end, they are going to guide you in the right direction whether or not it feels right at the time.

Final Thoughts

We know that as you read this book you might have been thinking, "Are these guys serious?" We also know that it may be next to impossible for you to follow and adopt each and every piece of advice that we've given you in this book. What we hope, however, is that you can pick and choose from the strategies and practices that we've described and that they will help you experience great success throughout your high school careers. You will need to find your own way; the way that is comfortable for you and fits your personality and character. But take it from us: Studying successful people who have come before you and learning from them is how many of the most successful people in the world got their start.

We want you to live a high school life that is enjoyable, interesting, fulfilling, and productive. The strategies and practices that successful students employ can help you make the best of your high school career. Remember that your parents, however annoying or intrusive, are only doing what they think is the best thing for you and your future. Most of the time, we have to warn you, they will be right. Listen to them and work with them.

Also, remember that your high school is full of adults who are there to support and guide you as you make your way through your high school experience. Lean on them! They have years of experience and insight into what you are facing and can prove to be an invaluable resource. You are not inconveniencing them by asking them for help. It is what they are paid to do!

Finally, we hope that you make memories that last a lifetime while you are in high school. Believe it or not, these four years will go by faster than you ever can imagine.

Take advantage of each opportunity for growth. We wish you the best of luck!

Resources for High School Students

One of the great advantages you have at your disposal as students in the twenty-first century are excellent online resources designed to help you experience success in school and beyond. We have collected some of these resources for you in this section, but remember, links and websites change often, so don't hesitate to search around on the internet on your own to find new and updated resources. There are a great number of online resources to help students navigate through their high school careers. Naturally, you'll want to visit the web home of your own school and school district to find out what resources in your own area have been provided for you. Remember, it is in the school and district's best interest for every student to receive the best support possible so they will experience high school success. You will find resources, tutorials, and services that you never knew existed if you only look.

ACADEMIC RESOURCES

As freshmen in high school, you will likely experience your first need for online resources in the area of "academics." It is common for young high school students to hit road blocks or obstacles to learning in the first year. Also, you may find that the teacher who you would like to meet with is unavailable due to meetings, coaching or club sponsor assignments, etc., which often take up after school time. Online resources, such as the ones listed below, may be your best bet for help.

High School Ace
High School Ace is a guide to some of the best free educational websites for teens. It is sponsored by QuizHub.com.
www.highschoolace.com

Finding Dulcinea – Librarian of the Internet
This great website can help students do research on just about any

topic. There are links to math, language arts, history, science...you name it. It will change how you search the web and will help you learn how to find anything on the internet using quality websites. You'll become a smarter, savvier searcher.
www.findingdulcinea.com/

Hippo Campus
Hippo Campus is a project of the Monterey Institute for Technology and Education (MITE). The goal of Hippo Campus is to provide high-quality, multimedia content on general education subjects to high school and college students free of charge. Students can visit this site to get help in virtually every subject taught in high school. The content is provided by some of the finest colleges and universities in the world.
www.hippocampus.org

coolmath.com
This site offers some quick refreshers and hints at just about every math topic taught in high school, from pre-algebra through calculus. Don't mind the cheesy graphics – the content can be really helpful to a student in need of help!
www.coolmath.com

math.com
Here is another resource for math students who are struggling with math concepts. This site breaks each subject down into it sub-content and provides detailed explanations of solutions.
www.math.com

American Chemical Society: High School Student Programs and Resources
If you're a high school student with a strong interest in chemistry or would like to pursue chemistry in college, ACS provides programs and resources for you.
http://portal.acs.org

MathBits.com

MathBits.com is devoted to offering fun, yet challenging, lessons and activities in secondary (and college level) mathematics and computer programming for students.
http://mathbits.com

Student.com

This site has a wealth of material on college search process, test preparation programs, student loans, scholarships, and grants, as well as a social network for students to belong to.
www.student.com

PBS *It's My Life*

It's My Life is funded by the Corporation for Public Broadcasting to create safe educational online media activities for teenagers. Parents and teens can read informative articles, share stories, play games, and get advice from experts.
pbskids.org/itsmylife/parents/resources/highschool.html

***ProofWriter*™— The Online Writing Tool**

This service for students provides quick analysis of written documents along with helpful grammar, usage, mechanics and style rules designed to increase learning and encourage better writing skills.
www.proofwriter.ets.org

RESOURCES FOR POST-SECONDARY PLANNING

We know life after high school seems like a lifetime away, but it is not. It will be here sooner than you can imagine. Here are some great sites to look at while you are completing your Post-Secondary Plan in conjunction with your parents. Also, as you continue along your journey, you can come back to these sites as you refine your plan.

Nelnet

This site provides information for planning and financing education along with planning careers.
www.nelnet.com

Office of Postsecondary Education
Provides information for students preparing for their future.
www.ed.gov/students/prep/college/index.html

Mapping Your Future
This site provides students and parents with information on financial strategies, career options, and college planning.
www.mappingyourfuture.org

PREPARATION FOR COLLEGE ENTRANCE EXAMINATIONS

As ninth graders, you might think that the time when you are going to have to sit for hours taking long college entrance exams are a long way off, but in truth it is never too soon to begin to prepare for these very important and high-stakes exams. Below are sites that provide good information about the tests and even free test preparation.

ACT
Provides information about registering for the ACT test; and provides students practice tests to prepare for the ACT examination.
www.act.org

The College Board
This site provides information about registering for the SAT test, and provides help to students who want to prepare for the SAT.
www.collegeboard.com

Educational Testing Service
Provides practice tests and resources for parents and students who are interested in Advanced Placement (AP), PSAT, and other educational tests.
www.ets.org

Number2.com
This is an great, totally free test preparation site that will get you ready for the SAT and ACT tests. All you have to do is sign on, and an account will

be created for you to help you get ready for these important exams. They will even email you to remind you to get to work preparing for the tests.
www.number2.com

COLLEGE SEARCH INFORMATION

You are likely to begin discussions about where you might like to go to college with school officials only in your junior, or in some cases, the beginning of your senior year. We think this is far, far too late. Take some time to visit some of the great college search sites early in your high school career to get an idea of what it will take for you to get into various colleges and universities.

College Opportunities OnLine (COOL)
This site allows prospective students to see and compare profiles of colleges and universities across the nation.
www.nces.ed.gov/collegenavigator

College Portrait
Provides accountability data on institutional performance; sponsored by the National Association of State Universities and Land-Grant Colleges and by the American Association of State Colleges and Universities.
www.collegeportraits.org

College.gov
Site designed by students and sponsored by the U.S. Department of Education.
www.college.gov/wps/portal

CollegeNET
Provides links for college searches, applications, and scholarships.
http://www.collegenet.com

FastWeb
Registration required; provides searches for colleges, scholarships,

jobs, and internships.
www.fastweb.com

GoCollege
This site provides resources for admissions, education options, college survival, and financial aid.
www.gocollege.com

Thompson Peterson's
Provides search tools for colleges and universities, articles, and resources to help find the right school.
www.petersons.com

RESOURCES ABOUT PAYING FOR COLLEGE AND FINANCIAL AID INFORMATION

It is never too soon to start thinking about how you will be able to pay for college. This valuable education does not come cheap – most college educations cost upwards of $120,000 to complete a Bachelor's degree. Don't give up! There are a number of sites that can show you how anyone can put together the financial package that will allow them to get the education they will need to have the best future. Planning is everything, however, so start early.

"Cash for College" Program - N.A.S.F.A.A.
Provides information on paying for college and applying for financial aid.
www.nasfaa.org/Home.asp

College Answer
This site from Sallie Mae offers college planning tools in both English and Spanish.
www.collegeanswer.com/index.jsp

College Is Possible
A service offered by the American Council on Education, this site provides parents and students resources for paying, preparing, and choos-

ing the right college.
www.acenet.edu/AM/Template.cfm?Section=CIP1

Federal Student Financial Assistance
Provides information on preparing for and funding education beyond high school.
www.studentaid.ed.gov/PORTALSWebApp/students/english/index.jsp

Fund Finder (by The College Board)
Provides information on how to save or pay for college and financial aid basics.
www.collegeboard.com/student/pay/add-it-up/index.html

Free Application for Federal Student Aid (FAFSA)
This site show students and parents to how fill out the FAFSA with step-by-step instructions.
www.fafsa.ed.gov

Free Scholarship Searches
Provides links to more than 40 free online scholarship search sites.
www.college-scholarships.com/free_scholarship_searches.htm

National Student Loan Data System (NSLDS)
This site allows you to check your student loan records; you will need your FAFSA PIN to access your NSLDS records.
www.nslds.ed.gov/nslds_SA

Scholarship Experts
Requires registration and provides free scholarship searches.
www.scholarshipexperts.com/

Scholarships.com
Provides links for scholarship searches, college searches, and scholarship providers.
www.scholarships.com

The Smart Student Guide to Financial Aid
This site provides information on scholarships, loans, military aid, and saving for college.
www.finaid.org

Index